2020

The YEAR the Earth Stood Still

Joe Calitri

PAGE PUBLISHING
Conneaut Lake, PA

First originally published by Page Publishing 2024

ISBN 979-8-89157-898-2 (pbk)
ISBN 979-8-89157-910-1 (digital)

Printed in the United States of America

CONTENTS

PROLOGUE

It began as most other years have. Winter was gaining momentum with increasing snowfall and frigid temperatures. Leftists, Democrats, and their *fake news* media lackeys continued to libel, slander, and falsely accuse President Trump and his supporters of endless wrong-doings, accelerating the attacks they had launched the moment he first announced his presidential candidacy. There was something else in the atmosphere though—an odd kind of static—a strange, unpleasant sensation. The year 2020 was on the verge of becoming one for the record books, in a very unpleasant way.

Within the first weeks of January, a major world event began to unfold. Government authorities in the United States and other nations announced the appearance of a new, dangerous viral infection, which had the potential, they warned, to expand into a pandemic. As February approached, declarations of public health emergencies exploded across the planet. People were understandably anxious, but far too many Americans became irrationally frightened.

Legions of scientists and medical professionals rushed to identify the disease, labeled COVID-19, SARS-2, and to design methods to combat its effects on human populations. President Trump directed pharmaceutical companies and research laboratories to focus their resources on developing therapeutic treatments and possible vaccines against what was advertised as one of the world's most debilitating health crises. Ultimately, though, COVID-19 was exposed as arguably the greatest hoax and fraud ever perpetrated by sinister forces against humanity, a *plandemic*. I'll explore more of the political and social dysfunction that arose from this event in chapters to come.

The term *The Government* is often misused in conversation. A government is not an entity or a singularity but a collection of elected and appointed officials given the responsibilities of maintaining the well-being of civil populations. Someone who screams "*The Government* did [this or that]" or "Don't believe anything *The Government* tells you" is ranting at empty space. Complaints and grievances need to be directed at specific political authorities. It's fair to say that a majority of public officials controlling federal, state, and local governments either succumbed to or ignored the silent coup against the Trump administration being orchestrated by radical, corrupt Leftist operatives. They offered little or no opposition and expressed even less concern for the well-being of American citizens.

A while back, I coined a convenient term, *The Collective*, to describe the cast of subversives responsible for this fantastically disturbing plot and for the multitude of incidents that negatively impacted people worldwide. *The Collective* is comprised of Democrats, Leftists, Socialists, Progressives, Communists, Marxists, Globalists, and useful idiots who blindly subscribe to these mindsets. They all share the same origin, Liberalism. Over time, populations have gradually become indifferent to or tolerant of behavior that was once considered to be uncivil or offensive. This fostered an anything-goes tsunami that has resulted in decades of cultural and political rot.

Were you alive and cognitively functioning in the year 2020? Did you or any of your family members or friends contract the *China virus*? Were you inconvenienced by outrageous mask mandates, forced business closings, or shuttered schools and churches? Did you lose your job? Read on, and think back to the most impactful events that far too many Americans were subjected to. These things all happened in 2020, truly a year from hell!

Liberalism is an ideology. Conservatism is a way of life. The difference between modern Liberalism and Conservatism is the first one believes that government is owner and distributor of freedom and rights, while the other maintains that government exists to protect the rights and freedoms Man is born with.

—Mark Levin

1

A Most Sinister Scheme

Life-changing occurrences during the year 2020 combined to form a nightmare of Satanic proportions. I cannot imagine that any single human being or group of conspirators is intelligent enough and possesses sufficient power to plan, organize, and implement worldwide control over most of the population. Such an effort would dwarf all the military operations launched by every country in the history of mankind, combined! A supernatural evil must have infiltrated our mortal world.

Many observant, analytically minded folks echoed my sentiments as pieces of this sinister puzzle began to appear. *The Collective* has often and openly expressed its mad desire to dominate the world's population. There is no secret to their aspirations, from Margaret Sanger's birth control activism in the early twentieth century to the creation of the modern-day organization, planned parenthood, and globalist enthusiasts. Proponents of this ideology began voicing legitimate concerns about the effects of overpopulation on food supplies, potable water sources, and a breathable atmosphere free from contaminants. However, hidden within their admonitions were mechanisms to bestow on world leaders the sole authority to determine which populations needed to be culled, who would live, and who would have to be eliminated. What better way to impact humanity than to infect it with a dangerous disease?

Introducing, the *China virus*! As power-hungry government leaders accelerated warnings and manufactured an assortment of public health crises, terrified people flocked to these same corrupt entities for salvation. On the other hand, more rational folks began expressing skepticism and legitimate concerns. Agenda-driven officials would have none of this though.

Rather than entertain any opposition to their subterfuge, tyrannical political leaders were quick to impose their wills on entire populations in the forms of mandates, quarantines, and oppressive dictates. Outside of observing life in third-world countries and Communist-run nations, when have Americans ever experienced such authoritarianism? When in American history have patriots ever acceded to such outrageous demands without offering resistance?

Once millions of trepid people accepted invasive therapies being used on *China virus* patients, in the form of ventilators, respirators, and ineffective medicines, *The Collective's* scheme settled firmly in place. Too many folks stood idly by as virus victims, primarily elderly, were transferred from hospitals to outside healthcare facilities. There was no adequate treatment available or administered in these centers. Patients' families were denied access to visitation. Communication between the affected parties, company staff, and medical professionals was limited at best. Thousands of patients died unnecessarily due to this warehousing, confinement, and lack of care. Could this have been the beginning of a population control experiment?

Has any American ever heard of a safe and efficient drug like ivermectin actually being banned by government officials for use against a particular disease? Is anyone aware of a problematic concoction like remdesivir being forcefully injected into patients without their knowledge or consent? Nefarious authorities actually prevented physicians from prescribing and pharmacists from dispensing ivermectin, despite evidence of its effectiveness. Infected people who were fortunate enough to acquire ivermectin reported its benefits in combating the *China virus*, while many remdesivir victims suffered debilitating aftereffects, including blood clots, amputations, and, in some cases, death. Do these actions qualify as more population control exercises?

Medical care providers continued to experiment with an assortment of treatments for virus-infected people, while pharmaceutical companies struggled to produce vaccines. As 2020 progressed, petrified folks began clamoring for a cure to the *China virus* so much so that they voluntarily allowed themselves to be injected with dangerous, untested medicines. All along, the *fake news* media censored any mention of patients who recovered from these infections using sensible, time-honored treatments of vitamin D, zinc, and remedies that boosted their immune systems. Meanwhile, the globalists goose-stepped onward.

When the lines of vaccination volunteers began to shorten, authoritarians tried to implement vaccine mandates, forcing people to comply under the threat of losing their employments. Government fascists and their willing accomplices in business and industry ignored the God-given constitutional rights of Americans in the interest of furthering the Left's agenda.

This malevolent, supernatural plot achieved another fascinating goal through deceit and trickery. As problematic as the *China virus* was, it didn't have the potential to cause as much damage to populations as the vaccine cocktails did. Ingeniously, the plotters and their useful idiot lackeys succeeded in frightening enough people into receiving the vaccines. After exhaustive investigations by credible sources, those drugs, it turns out, were the causes of more deaths and injuries than was the disease. What a brilliant plan, herding people into expediting their own demises?

The *China virus* pandemic madness was unbearable to say the least, but another reprehensible plot lingered in the background, biding its time. *The Collective* capitalized on the plethora of quarantines, travel restrictions, and business closings to manipulate the 2020 US presidential election. They skirted the law and the Constitution just enough to force mass voting by mail. Never before had the country witnessed the installation of hundreds of ballot drop boxes, bulk mailing of unsecured ballots, or ballot harvesting. Leftists paralyzed the nation with a phony pandemic, restricted an unprecedented number of American liberties, and obtained physical control over millions of ballots. They knew that the Democrat candidate for president had no chance of victory in a fair and honest election, so theft and fraud became their only options.

The objectives of this demonic plan were manyfold. Population control was, and still is, a priority for lunatic Leftists. Trump derangement syndrome likely afflicted more people than the *China virus* did. The Left's hatred of President Trump is immeasurable and uncontrollable, yet their rage is not directed solely at Trump but at Conservatives, Republicans, Christians, the US Constitution, the Bible, and common sense. The 2016 election of President Trump was a mountainous obstacle for *The Collective*. He and his supporters had to be destroyed, even at the cost of American culture, values, and way of life.

2

The China Virus

Why do I insist on calling this disease the *China virus*? Because it was released by (wait for it) CHINA, after allegedly being created in some insidious laboratory in Ukraine! President Trump used this applicable term in response to a question from a snarky reporter who was obviously trying to provoke him into making some kind of misstatement. I, too, began referring to COVID-19 as the *China virus* around the same time as President Trump did. The moniker is certainly appropriate. Whenever I used the term *China virus* in conversation with a pansy Leftist, I received that typical stare of incredulity. How dare I blame the Communist Chinese government for any wrongdoing?

The outbreak of this strange but somewhat familiar disease was inarguably the most impactful event of 2020. The fraudulent theft of the American presidential election by Leftist Democrats was a close second, an aftereffect of the ersatz pandemic.

On January 9, 2020, the World Health Organization announced that a dangerous coronavirus, COVID-19, had emerged from Wuhan, China, and was spreading across the globe with amazing speed.

The first case of COVID-19 in the United States was reported by the CDC on January 21. Ten days later, President Trump imposed travel restrictions preventing foreign nationals from entering the United States if they had visited China within the previous two weeks. He later expanded the travel ban to include six other countries: Eritrea, Kyrgyzstan, Myanmar, Nigeria, Sudan, and Tanzania.

In a matter of a few months, nearly the entire planet was forced into a state of lockdown. American government authorities labored to convince the general public that self-quarantining was necessary to prevent the spread of this virus. The initial explanation given by political leaders and healthcare professionals was that fifteen days of isolation would be needed to *flatten the curve* on graphs that detailed the disease's progress. However, clear-thinking folks sensed a more ominous scheme in the making. The unopposed fifteen-day quarantine quickly evolved into an indefinite, tyrannical abuse of constitutional and basic human rights, which, in turn, crushed the US economy and destroyed thousands of private businesses, careers, and employments. The procedures taken to combat the *plandemic* disrupted millions of lives and ended millions more. A mass sanitizing effort was implemented. *Social distancing* protocols of maintaining six feet of space between persons became widely imposed, and the wearing of face coverings in public was being rigidly and unreasonably enforced.

There's no arguing the fact that this disease was legitimately dangerous. It was debilitating for infected people and definitely problematic for those with compromised immune systems or comorbidity issues. How it spread among the populations of the world is the subject of widespread speculation and debate. The truth may or may not ever be discovered or accurately explained.

For generations, Americans have been fortunate to have a network of local, state, and federal health services keeping them updated on major outbreaks of diseases and infections. Vigilant folks have long been paying close attention to seasonal influenza updates. Most people are grateful to receive warnings about contagions like tuberculosis, Ebola, smallpox, and an assortment of animal-named flu viruses in advance of their appearances. Pneumonia is an infection that always concerns medical professionals and patients because of its potentially deadly effects. Rational, factually informed people, however, concluded that the *China virus* would not be any more threatening than other such diseases, and they took reasonable, not irrational precautions.

From its outset, many health officials and political authorities raced to make comparisons between the *China virus* and the 1918 Spanish flu pandemic, which killed millions across the globe. They published unscientific predictions of similar death tolls from the *China virus*. Quite conveniently, many self-appointed experts and their rump-swabs in the *fake news* media pushed the pandemic narrative as forcefully as they could. However, the *China virus* certainly was not comparable to the bubonic plague that killed an estimated twenty-five million Europeans between AD 1347 and AD 1351, nor was it as overpowering as the fictional Motaba virus from the movie *Outbreak*, which was portrayed as being 100% fatal.

President Trump did not hesitate to take action to protect the American people from this invasive disease. He created Operation Warp Speed, which encouraged researchers, pharmaceutical companies, and medical equipment providers to concentrate on developing medicines to combat the virus, along with stockpiling protective equipment and lifesaving devices used to therapeutically treat infected patients. When state governors, city mayors, and government solons begged the Trump administration for surgical masks, ventilators, hospital beds, and staffing assistance, the president responded immediately. He ensured that medical supplies were distributed in a timely fashion. He dispatched the Army Corps of Engineers to construct makeshift hospitals in critical areas and even directed the Navy hospital ships *USNS Mercy* and *USNS Comfort* to the epicenters of escalating infection, Los Angeles, and New York City, respectively. In the face of heroic efforts on the part of so many healthcare providers, federal agencies, and civilian volunteers, *The Collective* ratcheted up its attacks against President Trump, downplaying and demeaning his every accomplishment.

In December 2020, the FDA fraudulently issued an Emergency Use Authorization (EUA) for dangerous and untested COVID-19 vaccines that were, in fact, DNA-altering gene-mutation injections that spread millions of spike prions throughout a victim's vascular system, cleansing organs, heart, and brain.

Unfortunately, before the end of his presidency, Trump was caught between the proverbial rock and a hard place. If he had ignored this biological menace threatening the American people, he would have been labeled heartless and incompetent. But by motivating drug companies and laboratories to manufacture some kind of preventative against the *China virus*, he stood to bear the brunt of any negative optics. Throughout his initial response, President Trump received inadequate information and recommendations, deliberately or unintentionally, from trusted advisors. He was forced to advocate these vaccines to the public to assuage their fear and angst. The horrific side effects of such untested medications ultimately superseded those of the virus itself as time progressed. Though President Trump spearheaded the effort to create *China virus* vaccines, I know of no particular blame assigned to him for their impact on the American people. Incredibly, the perpetrators of this attack against the United States waged a ceaseless campaign to manipulate people into being vaccinated, going as far as to issue unconstitutional vaccine mandates. Resistance to this authoritarianism prevented many Americans from accessing public facilities and events, airline services, and hospitals and, in some cases, resulted in people being terminated from their positions of employment!

3

Outbreak in the Family

Early in December 2020, the *China virus* found its way into my loved ones' relatively peaceful lives. My wife and I had been living with our daughter's family since 2016 to provide in-home childcare for our two granddaughters, aged five and one at the time. After some investigation, we discovered that our five-year-old had contracted the disease from an infected schoolteacher. Not surprisingly, the virus spread quickly through our household. The children were first to show symptoms. Their affliction was relatively mild, and the girls' natural immunity helped them fully recover in a few days. We four adults were not as fortunate. The virus hit us hard with effects similar to those of influenza, with unrelenting fatigue being the most impactful symptom. Fortunately, our nurse practitioner daughter quickly prescribed high doses of zinc and vitamin D for us, a combination that was reportedly effective in minimizing side effects and stimulating recovery. She also encouraged my wife and me to obtain antibiotic Z-pack medication from our primary care provider as a precaution against pneumonia. Despite the seriousness of our infections, my daughter, her husband, my wife, and I returned to health in sixteen days, thanks to our robust immune systems and some timely therapeutic medicines.

Some of us suffered a temporary loss of taste and smell, and others dealt with sinus problems, but none of us was burdened by respiratory difficulty, coughing, or headaches. We all were overcome by energy-draining fatigue, the likes of which we had never encountered before. The simple act of climbing stairs made me crave a nap in order to recover.

In no way am I trying to downplay the danger of this disease. Countless numbers of people around the world died as a result of the *China virus* exacerbating comorbidity health issues. Evidence suggests, though, that authority figures made decisions and issued directives that resulted in many of these deaths. Infected patients who were subjected to invasive ventilators, transferred from hospitals to nursing homes, and prevented from receiving proven, life-saving medicines might have survived, had they been treated therapeutically instead of experimentally.

Within weeks of the *China virus* outbreak, it had become apparent that the standard practice of putting patients on mechanical ventilation was a death sentence. Statistics showed 76.4% of infected people aged eighteen to sixty-five in New York City who were placed on ventilators expired. The mortality rate was 97.2% in victims over age sixty-five.

The recommendation to place virus patients on ventilation as an initial response came from the corrupt World Health Organization, which made the decision allegedly based on advice from doctors in China. Incredibly, venting *China virus* patients was not encouraged on the basis of increased survival but to safeguard healthcare workers by isolating the virus inside the vent machine.

According to the agency, treatment needed to be rapidly escalated to immediate mechanical ventilation. However, the notion of protecting healthcare providers at the expense of patient outcome was concealed from the public. WHO officials maintained that using less invasive positive air pressure machines could result in the spread of infectious respiratory excretions. Simply put, these bureaucrats deceitfully sentenced patients to death in order to save medical staff and other, presumably uninfected, patients.

Accumulated information determined that approximately 10,000 patients died from the *China virus* in New York City hospitals after being put on ventilators in the spring of 2020. The death rate continued to rise among younger people in suburban areas, who were at low risk of succumbing to the virus. There were also massive spikes in deaths among younger individuals who were at low risk of dying from the virus, possibly due to being placed on mechanical ventilation.

On March 31, 2020, Mount Sinai Health System critical care specialist Dr. Cameron Kyle-Sidell warned that "we must change what we are doing if we want to save as many lives as possible." Sidell insisted that medical practitioners were "treating the wrong disease" and criticized the use of ventilators on infected patients.

4

The Race for a Cure

With the *China virus* accelerating across the United States, President Trump launched Operation Warp Speed, a directive to pharmaceutical companies and drug manufacturers to expedite the creation of a vaccine to combat the disease. He was forced into a very unenviable position. A virus defense was desperately needed, but it was not medically or scientifically possible to safely synthesize such drugs in so short a time. The disease already had a death grip on humanity. President Trump engaged the attempt though. Still, he was vilified by lunatic Leftists for his every action. If he had not taken steps to commence development of a vaccine, he would have been accused of abandoning the American people in a time of need. It was a no-win situation.

When companies like Pfizer and Johnson & Johnson finally produced *China virus* vaccines, their drugs received mixed reviews. In October 2020, vice presidential candidate Kamala Harris stated, "If the public health professionals, if Dr. Fauci, if the doctors tell us we should take it, I'll be the first in line to take it, absolutely." In the same breath, she insinuated that if Donald Trump said people should be vaccinated, she would refuse to take it. After the 2020 presidential election fraud and the mock inauguration of Joe Biden, these exact same vaccines, created during the Trump administration, were touted and encouraged by the likes of Harris. What had changed besides the players? Nothing!

Government officials aggressively advertised these drugs and pushed them on people worldwide. Throngs of eager recipients began falling over each other in a rush to be vaccinated. Meanwhile, pensive folks were seeing red flags and raising alarms. Over the decades, mankind accepted inoculations against polio, smallpox, influenza, and other dangerous diseases. Those of us who were cognizant of the details that led to creation of these medicines and the time involved to ensure their safety and effectiveness became very skeptical of the unusually swift production of *China virus* vaccines.

The decisions to implement draconian restrictions were made in most countries by a small group of self-anointed experts and policymakers with enormous but secure salaries, without considering the needs of disadvantaged populations, self-employed businesspeople who lost their ability to provide for themselves and their families, and many others who were irreparably harmed by these measures.

This approach significantly degraded the practice of medicine, setting it back generations to the days of medical paternalism. Authoritarians violated ethical rules that govern public policy. The measures they took did not meet any standards of effectiveness, necessity, or proportionality.

Under the label *state of emergency*, scientific and medical researchers abandoned basic principles of open discussion, critical skepticism, and expressions of doubt, as well as the highest quality of unbiased research.

The Collective (remember, Democrats, Leftists, Socialists, Progressives, Communists, Marxists, Anarchists, and their useful idiots) created essentially a *vaccine slave state—medical martial law!*

There is absolutely no need for vaccines to extinguish the pandemic. I've never heard of such nonsense talk about vaccines. You do not vaccinate people who aren't at risk from a disease. You also don't set about planning to vaccinate millions of fit and healthy people with a vaccine that hasn't been extensively tested on human subjects.

—Dr. Michael Yeadon, Former Vice President
and Chief Scientist of Pfizer

5

Rise of the Mandates

Government officials maliciously stole our freedoms!

Fear is the most effective motivator of human behavior, and it played a most crucial role in the *China virus* crisis. Many of the world's governments learned nothing from history. They morally failed their respective populations by using propaganda to intimidate and terrorize the public while ignoring established norms and protocols to empower the citizens during emergencies. The spreading of anxiety and depression through vile propaganda took a heavy toll on the public.

Officials assured the American people that they would only be required to follow mandated guidelines for fifteen days in order to flatten the charted curve of the *China virus* infection rate. Bureaucrats initially urged folks to remain in their homes, limit their traveling, wear face masks when in public, and practice *social distancing*, remaining at least six feet away from other people. Most Americans accepted those requirements and cooperated with the strategy. That fifteen-day time period soon dragged into a year of misery, and as of this book's publication, *The Collective* still has not completely released its virus-related political stranglehold on the United States.

If authorities had been reasonable enough to simply encourage or strongly recommend actions to prevent the spread of the *China virus*, it's likely that people would have accepted directions without reservations. Unfortunately, encouragement and recommendations swiftly changed to orders, mandates, and a level of tyranny that most of us had never experienced.

The United States Constitution was designed to acknowledge, guarantee, and protect the God-given rights that all Americans are gifted with. It is a document that strictly limits the power of elected officials over the people, essentially telling government authorities what they can and cannot do. Leftists would have everyone believe that the reverse is true: that the Constitution empowers the government to control the people. Americans *do not* lose their constitutional rights for *any* reason, not during war, pestilence, or natural disasters, and they definitely do not lose them because of a *plandemic*.

Some corrupt political leaders even imposed curfews and travel restrictions in populated areas and ordered law enforcement officers to request from civilians their *papers*, i.e., *vaccine passports*, in order to approve their movements.

Rampant despotism fell upon the American people early in 2020 as bureaucrats began ordering private businesses to close their doors to the public. Many establishment owners refused to shut down, defending their rights and those of employees who were being forcefully prevented from earning their livelihoods. In retaliation, corrupt Leftist officials ordered law enforcement agencies to physically lock down businesses and, in some cases, arrest the owners, even though these individuals had not violated any laws! Such oppression is what changes a representative republic into a police state!

In May 2020, Rick Savage, owner of Sunday River Brewing in Bethel, Maine, initially complied with the closure demand but quickly realized the damage that would befall his establishment and its employees if the restaurant remained closed. He defied the order and reopened, despite threats of repercussion from government officials. State authorities began issuing fines against Savage. They rescinded his operational permit and revoked his liquor license without just cause or due process. Patrons and friends began donating money to a GoFundMe account to mitigate fines and legal fees as Savage fought courageously to keep his restaurant open.

Does anyone possessing even a modicum of reason and common sense believe that this kind of third-world dictatorship is acceptable in the United States of America?

Later, in July 2020, two New Jersey fitness center owners who repeatedly reopened in defiance of that state's virus lockdown were arrested. Atilis Gym owners in Bellmawr—Ian Smith, thirty-three, of Delanco Township, and Frank Trumbetti, fifty-one, of Williamstown—were charged with contempt and violation of a *disaster control act*, according to the Camden County Prosecutor's Office. A bizarre ordinance like this is *not law*. It was a haphazard order approved by corrupt state legislators, and it most definitely violated the rights of Americans under the US Constitution. Governors do have the legal authority to impose certain mandates upon state entities and within state facilities, but neither a governor nor any county, city, or town official has the wherewithal to enforce such dictates on the public.

The two owners continually railed against Governor Phil Murphy's executive order amid the *China virus* madness and even sued lawmakers, claiming their constitutional rights were violated when they were forced to close their South Jersey gym. In a post on the gym's Facebook page, Smith attacked the governor for *flexing his little tyrant muscles.*

While hundreds of small businesses were forcibly shuttered, many large companies whose managements were regular donors to Democrat political interests, for example, Walmart and Target, were allowed to keep their shopping centers open. Was there a quid pro quo in this arrangement? Stores that were allowed to remain open were given strict guidelines. They were ordered to display signs mandating *social distancing* and requiring the wearing of face coverings. Owners were put in the unenviable position of enforcing government mandates upon their customers or risk fines, closure, or other dictatorial punishment.

Government scofflaws then anointed themselves with the authority to impose *forced* vaccinations upon the American people.

There is *no* provision or allowance in the Constitution or any other legal document that grants such power to bureaucrats. For generations, control freaks have danced through halls of justice in search of ideological judges who would validate such authority, but jurists could only issue opinions. No courtroom edict supersedes the God-given constitutional rights of American citizens.

In Tarrant County, Texas, where I reside, a judge made just such a decision. He declared that the local health department had the legal authority to order certain businesses to close their doors; face masks must be worn by everyone, indoors or outdoors; and that people were required to *social distance* at least six feet apart in public. The proprietors of establishments that were allowed to remain open were involuntarily assigned to be *mandate police* and were expected to enforce such orders. Government officials had the audacity to impose fines on business owners who failed to comply with the new rules.

My personal dentist and dermatologist confided in me that they feared having their operating licenses revoked if they did not force their patients to wear *obedience masks* while in their offices. I respected their concerns, but I steadfastly refused to wear a face covering, citing my constitutional rights and displaying a badge that explained those rights. Both medical professionals made accommodations for me by escorting me into their respective offices through employee entrances and keeping me more or less out of sight of other patients. My principles never allowed me to accede to illegal mandates, and they never will.

These ridiculous orders quickly expanded into hospitals and healthcare centers, large companies, and government agencies, mandating that employees submit to forced vaccinations of untested and problematic drugs or be subject to discipline, up to and including termination.

Fascists aligned with *The Collective* ordered schools and churches to be closed. They audaciously limited the number of people allowed to attend weddings, funerals, and other public gatherings.

At no time in history have the people forcing others into compliance been the *good guys!*

Forced vaccinations and vaccine passports to enter buildings and businesses, in conjunction with media censorship and increasingly restrictive unconstitutional laws, were all obvious signs that the very freedoms so many Americans fought and died to protect and uphold were being eroded.

Forced or coerced vaccination is a violation of:

1. The Nuremberg Code
2. UNESCO Universal Declaration on
Bioethics and Human Rights (art. 6).
3. UN International Covenant on Civil
and Political Rights (art. 7).
4. UN Universal Declaration of Human Rights (art. 3).

—James Lewis, Twitter, May 1, 2021

6

Deadly Lockdowns

For the first time in the history of medicine, bureaucrats established the definition of a *case* for an infectious respiratory disease based on a laboratory test without considering the symptoms to verify the disease. The extremely sensitive PCR tests were able to identify remains of viral RNA from dead viruses, which likely resulted in an overdiagnosis of morbidity and mortality.

Most of the people who were considered to have died from the *China virus* were, in fact, adults who succumbed to the aggravation of their chronic preexisting conditions and not from the virus itself.

The inflated numbers did not reflect reality and only contributed to public fear and panic disseminated by the government tyrants.

A new study offers even more proof that lockdowns were deadly!

(Clear-thinking folks who didn't march in blind obedience to their Leftist Democrat masters knew this whole event was fraudulent from the beginning! That's why so many of us resisted the authoritarianism!)

In hopes of containing the pandemic, everyone across the country was forced to suffer through lockdown orders and closed schools and workplaces in the spring of 2020. In Democrat-controlled areas, many of these restrictions lingered into 2021, yet they didn't work. Far too many people contracted the *China virus* despite the lockdowns. More than a million Americans nonetheless died of the disease, and in a dark and ironic twist, most virus spreading actually happened in homes.

The unconstitutional quarantine restrictions obviously resulted in deadly consequences. Research from Casey B. Mulligan and Rob Arnett published in the journal *Inquiry* indicated that non-COVID deaths were highly elevated above expected trends in the United States in 2020 and 2021. The report found that over this period, approximately 97,000 Americans died annually (exclusive of *China virus* deaths) above the baseline trend. This is a statistic known as *excess deaths*.

These included 32,000 deaths from heart disease and hypertension, some of which may have been fueled by the disruption of healthcare services and healthy lifestyles caused by the *China virus* restrictions. In the meantime, deaths due to obesity-related illnesses, drug overdoses, and alcohol-related causes were all 12,000 to 15,000 above expected trends. These factors were exacerbated by the way virus lockdowns spawned social isolation, sedentary lifestyles, and mental health issues.

The data "point to a historic, yet largely unacknowledged, health emergency," the study concluded. "COVID-19 is deadly, but so were the draconian steps taken to mitigate it."

Analysts categorized the excess deaths by age, further clarifying the findings. Among adults aged eighteen to forty-four, total excess deaths (more than half of which were non-COVID related) were significantly elevated in an effort to portray the virus as deadlier than people realized. "While largely unharmed by the *China Virus*, their aggregate mortality rates increased 26 percent above previous trends," according to the study. "This is larger than the percentage increase in deaths for senior citizens, where the disease toll was largely concentrated, but has received scant notice."

The younger age group was always at very minimal risk of dying from the *China virus*. The fact that they saw so many excess deaths suggests that they were more adversely affected by the oppressive restrictions even though lockdowns were allegedly designed to protect other groups, particularly the elderly.

Not all of these deaths are directly attributable to *China virus* restrictions, but common sense and basic comparisons suggest that many of them certainly are. For example, Sweden took a much more hands-off approach to lockdowns, which actually resulted in fewer excess deaths than the scientific trends anticipated; in fact, there was no increase at all.

While many government public health experts still refuse to acknowledge these findings, the study proved that lockdowns generated far too many terminal patient outcomes. This study isn't an outlier; it's just one of many reaching similar conclusions.

The world was facing an ugly truth. Governments across the globe forced residents to quarantine. Authoritarian tyrants kept people from their livelihoods, closed their schools, and terrorized them into remaining indoors. This not only had fatal outcomes, but it caused immeasurable anguish for survivors and individuals fortunate enough to be spared from the disease.

The Collective and their useful idiots who forced these failed policies onto populations must be held accountable for their injustice and punished to the fullest extent of the law.

7

Economic Recession

The COVID-19 recession, also referred to as the Great Lockdown, was caused by a collective irrational reaction to the disease. It began in most parts of the world in February 2020. Many countries implemented states of confinement to prevent the spread of the orchestrated *China virus* pandemic, the global economy took a major hit, and the entire planet went into stages of financial decline. It was considered to be the biggest ongoing worldwide recession since the Great Depression of 1929.

After a year of global economic slowdown that saw stagnation of economic growth and consumer activity, the *China virus* lockdowns and other precautions taken in early 2020 drove the global economy into crisis. Within seven months, every advanced economy had fallen to recession.

The first major sign of this recession was the 2020 stock market crash, which saw major indices drop 20–30% in late February and March. Recovery began in early April 2020; by April 2022, the GDP for most major economies had either returned to or exceeded pre-pandemic levels, and many market indices recovered or even set new records by late 2022.

The recession saw unusually high and rapid increases in unemployment in many countries. By October 2020, more than ten million unemployment cases had been filed in the United States, swamping state computer systems and processes.

The United Nations predicted in April 2020 that global unemployment would wipe out 6.7% of working hours globally in the second quarter of 2020, equivalent to 195 million full-time workers. In some countries, unemployment was expected to be around 10%, with more severely affected nations from the pandemic having higher unemployment rates. Developing countries were also affected by a drop in remittances and exacerbation of pandemic-related famines.

The recession and the accompanying 2020 Russia-Saudi Arabia oil price war led to a drop in oil prices; the collapse of tourism, the hospitality industry, and the energy industry; and a downturn in consumer activity in comparison to the previous decade. The 2021–2022 global energy crisis was driven by a planetwide surge in demand as the world exited the early recession caused by the pandemic, particularly due to strong energy demand in Asia.

This was further exacerbated by the reaction to escalations of the Russo-Ukrainian war, culminating in the 2022 Russian invasion of Ukraine and the 2022 Russian debt default.

8

Mask Insanity!

Nothing—not the confusion, the blind panic, or the symptoms of the virus itself—enraged me more than the implementation of so-called mask mandates and observing so many people's frightened, irrational responses to them, not since viewing photographs of the Spanish flu outbreak in 1918 had I ever seen so many insecure folks covering their faces with some kind of cloth. Images from China and Japan have often shown throngs of citizens wearing medical masks as they went about their lives, but explanations for this behavior generally referred to air quality or weather-related respiratory conditions. Outside of the Orient, these scenes were rarely, if ever observed.

I have no formal training or experience in the medical field, but I was educated in the sciences through high school and college and studied in a pre-med program for a short time. My father was a well-respected and successful physician for more than half a century, and he forcefully encouraged me to follow in his profession. Such was not my calling, but I retained much of the medical knowledge I acquired. I was well aware that surgical masks were not designed to prevent virus transmission but to keep health practitioners' respiratory droplets from infecting patients undergoing medical treatments or procedures. Doctors and nurses might appear to be regularly utilizing such masks during hospital routines, but they do not wear them constantly. They are cognizant of the dangers of breathing excess carbon dioxide and inhaling cotton fibers for extended periods of time.

It's also common to see ambulatory patients who are recovering from medical procedures wearing surgical masks as they walk around hospital grounds. Such people usually have compromised immune systems, and they use those masks to safeguard themselves as much as possible against outside infections. What we don't see are medical facilities mandating that every person entering their establishments wear masks, not prior to the spring of 2020, anyway.

Early on in the *China virus* soap opera, my wife and I were shopping at a local grocery store in Texas and noticed several customers wearing face coverings. We were a bit taken aback since there was no need to wear such ridiculous items. To us, this mask-wearing was more a sign of fear and trepidation than one of common sense. An elderly couple suddenly and rudely confronted us and asked why we weren't wearing masks. I answered, "Because we're not stupid," and told them to mind their business. It was easy to see where this interaction was headed.

They became quite agitated, and the lady screeched, "Well, you're going to have to wear one because the judge said so!" (Refer to the previous chapter regarding the judge.)

In my usual inimitable manner, I told the couple to get away from us by exclaiming, "Fuck you, and fuck the judge!" It worked! They left!

Have you heard of any instances where a person *not* wearing a mask berated someone who *was* wearing one? Though such a confrontation could have happened somewhere, I have yet to find an example. No one I've questioned has heard of one, either. What does that indicate about the mindset and temperament of so many proponents of wearing *face diapers*? The weepers and whiners are quite likely Leftist Democrat ideologues. They were so terrified that they blindly believed the psychobabble from corrupt political pundits, all the *fake news* media lies and misinformation, and succumbed to *virtue posturing* and a feel-good mentality. Imagine what their reactions would have been if President Trump and Republican leaders had imposed such a mandate? Those people most likely would have rebelled against it!

Here are a few incidents of mask insanity that made headlines far and wide:

1. On July 27, 2020, a woman at a San Diego dog park pepper-sprayed a couple for not wearing masks. A video posted to Facebook by Ash Sherilynn O'Brien showed a woman with a dog waving a black object in a man's face. "What are you doing? You cannot be serious, you just— you just maced him," someone called out. O'Brien wrote on Facebook that she and her husband were eating lunch with their pug at Dusty Rhodes dog park when the woman started giving them the middle finger and calling them idiots for not having their masks on. O'Brien said the woman pointed the pepper spray at her first but only got some on her and then sprayed her husband. "That is me crying hysterically in the background because my innocent husband just got maced for no reason," O'Brien said of the video.

2. After a January 27, 2021, incident, Kourtland Perry said he was lucky to be alive after a store employee attacked him for not wearing a mask. "I was in shock. I was embarrassed," Perry told FOX 5's Deidra Dukes. "I lost money over this. I have staples in my head right now." Perry showed FOX 5 the injuries he said he received during the violent encounter with a worker at this Family Dollar on MLK Drive in southwest Atlanta on Tuesday morning. Perry told FOX 5 he stopped at the store on his way to work and forgot to put

on his mask before entering the business. A male employee confronted Perry for not wearing the face covering. Perry said, "He referred to the policy at the front. He said, 'You have to have a mask,' and I was trying to explain to him, I said, 'Yeah, I'm sorry I kind of forgot it in the midst of me rushing to work. I apologize.'" Perry said the man followed him to the checkout counter, hurling insults at him as the store manager tried to diffuse the situation. Perry decided he'd had enough. "In the midst of me leaving, this gentleman reaches into his waistband, grabbed a gun, and hit me in the back of my head with it," said Perry. Perry called the police. Medics transported the forty-year-old man to the hospital for treatment for a head wound. In the police report obtained by FOX 5, the responding officer states a store surveillance camera recorded the incident. An APD spokesman said the investigation is ongoing. Perry said the man pushed him out of the store after striking him, got in his car, and drove off. "I'm very concerned that this is going on because no one knew he had a weapon but him. He could've killed me, he could've killed an employee, he could've killed a child. This is alarming to me that this could happen," Perry said.

3. This August 1, 2020, report came from England's *The Guardian*. Paul Feeley has been abused four times for not wearing a mask on public transport. "I have a disability lanyard, which signifies I have a hidden disability. I tried to show it…And all I got back was a complete torrent of abuse." The most recent incident took place just after he first spoke to the *Observer* on Thursday. The abuse has made Feeley, who suffers from fibromyalgia, borderline personality disorder, and panic attacks, feel "extraordinarily angry, anxious and upset." He is unable to wear a face covering due to his medical conditions, and legally he is exempted—but he is now worried about travelling on buses and trams in his hometown of Manchester. "One

man said to me, 'If you can't wear a mask, you shouldn't be allowed out.'"

Incidents of "mask rage" are making disabled people who are unable to wear a covering fearful of going out in public, charities warn, as they call on the government today to raise awareness about the legitimate reasons many people cannot wear them.

The Collective is responsible for creating a war within a war simply by issuing an irrational mandate. Many people who bought into the falsehoods of face coverings protecting them from virus transmission became irrational and aggressive toward those who resisted wearing masks. Other folks were aware of the ineffectiveness of obedience masks and strenuously objected to dictates. Far too many knee-jerk reactionaries on both sides of this argument expressed their ire violently. All the while, lunatic Leftists smiled and gloated over successfully manufacturing another crisis.

Consider a historical similarity. Some people living in Nazi Germany during World War II were so intimidated by their persecutors that they reported strangers, friends, and even relatives, suspected of subversion, to government authorities. During the 2020 virus scare, there were numerous reports of comparably weak-minded people reporting others to officials for not wearing *obedience masks*. I'm not aware of anyone being arrested, tortured, or murdered for such civil disobedience, as so many suffered under the Nazis, but the analogy is valid. In both cases, civilians were so frightened of their oppressors that they willingly aided and abetted the evil rather than confronting and resisting it.

The real winners of this conflict were undoubtedly the entrepreneurs who capitalized on the insane demands for face coverings. Standard surgical masks quickly became unavailable in some areas, and so many folks resigned to wearing hardware store painting masks, stylish bandanas and scarves, and ragged strips of cloth to soothe their fears of the *China virus*. A few resourceful enterprisers began custom designing *obedience masks* bearing sports team logos, company symbols, catchy slogans, and even American flags, of all things. Despite the proven facts that none of these ridiculous face coverings prevented virus transmission, the people displaying them were now feeling doubly virtuous: "See, I'm wearing a mask because I obey authority and I really care!" The manufacturers of these face coverings must have made literal fortunes from sales.

I uncovered a report from the American Academy of Physicians and Surgeons that detailed, through honest and factual research, the inability of any common face mask to prevent virus transmission. According to credible medical professionals, one would have to wear a suit designed to protect against hazardous materials plus a self-contained breathing apparatus, free from outside contamination, in order to be completely shielded from viruses. I posted this study on social media and forwarded it to my e-mail contacts. Most folks were grateful for the information, but one female acquaintance responded, "Well, wearing a mask still might do some good!"

A once-very good friend submitted a number of ignorant encouragements on social media, insisting, "Wear your masks! Keep your distance! Don't be selfish!" Many years ago, this man described himself as a proud, Liberal Democrat. Somehow, I wasn't surprised that he supported a Leftist government mandate.

A potent aspect of psychological operations (psyops) that found its way into many people's cerebrums was the notion that someone who defied the unconstitutional mandates was in essence a killer who was responsible for *China virus* deaths, was inconsiderate and selfish, and cared nothing for other people's health and safety. These critics were ideologically stubborn and unwittingly hypocritical. They believed in the phony Leftist *pseudo-science.* They were comfortable thinking that *social distancing* would keep the virus at bay. They were convinced that face coverings protected them from infection. If their masks truly worked and saved wearers from the *China virus*, why would other folks be required to wear them as well? There would be no need for two people to wear masks when interacting; the masked person would be totally protected, while the unmasked individual would simply be taking his or her chances, making free will decisions, right? No one would be forcing his or her beliefs on anyone.

How much publicity was given to the irrefutable fact that wearing face coverings can adversely affect a person's health? If there was any, it was sparse or censored. People suffering from asthma, environmental allergies, or other respiratory difficulties are hard-pressed to breathe when their mouths and noses are covered. Was any government bureaucrat concerned about *those* people's rights?

The following are confirmed long-term side effects of wearing face masks:

1. Shortness of breath and lightheadedness.
2. "Activities that result in the expulsion of air, such as talking, yelling, singing and exercising can result in the accumulation of carbon dioxide between the face and the mask," says Dr. Lili Barsky. "These symptoms are seen due to increases in CO2 levels in your body," says Dr. Rashmi Byakodi. "Breathing over exhaled air that turns into carbon dioxide might make you feel dizzy."
3. Headaches.
4. "Long-term wearing of masks can result in prolonged and repeated episodes of headaches," says Dr. Byakodi. "Headaches may occur due to the band fitting around the head all day, stress from breathing through the mask, or slight changes in oxygen and carbon dioxide levels in the blood," says Dr. Leann Poston.
5. Acne.
6. "Re-wearing unwashed reusable masks or re-wearing disposable masks can lead to inhalation of dust, pollen, bacteria and other particle contaminants trapped within the mask material," says Dr. Barsky. This can clog your pores and cause breakouts, primarily around your chin.
7. Development of chronic dermatitis.
8. "In the case of surgical masks, the nonwoven fabric is made by using chemicals to bond the fibers together. Some people who have sensitive skin can break out and develop some form of dermatitis as a result of the repeated exposure," says Dr. Sanul Corrielus. "This can have long term consequences in terms of recurrence and scarring of the skin around the face."

9. A weakened immune system.
10. "There are studies indicating that low oxygen levels in the tissues (hypoxia) can suppress some aspects of the immune response," says Dr. Esteban Kosak. "Scientific investigations have proven that a prolonged denial of enough oxygen in the body can cripple the ability of our immune system to tackle infections which is even worse with older and younger people."
11. Skin wrinkles.
12. According to Viseslav Tonkovic-Capin, MD, dermatologist and editor at DermBoard, another effect of long-term face mask use is new patterns of skin wrinkling. It's best to stock up on some lotions and facial moisturizers.
13. Development of chronic respiratory conditions.
14. "In the case of the surgical masks which are made of nonwoven fabric, the exposure for some people can trigger an asthma-like inflammatory response in the lungs," says Dr. Corrielus. "This is likely due to the inhalation of the microfibers in the material that forms the masks." (Source MSNBC: https://www.msn.com/en-ca/health/medical/7-long-term-side-effects-of-wearing-face-masks/ss-BB15mSnO#image=2)

Consider a few more likelihoods:

1. If these face coverings were as effective in preventing virus transmissions as political authorities claim, why would healthy people need to be forced to wear them? Wouldn't those with compromised immune systems or comorbidity issues be safe enough wearing their own masks?
2. If government officials simply recommended or urged Americans to wear face masks instead of dictating a requirement, wouldn't there have been more cooperation and fewer histrionics?
3. If there was no resistance to tyrannical mandates of mask wearing, socially distancing from other people, and closing

businesses, schools, and churches, there would have been no limits to governmental control over the population.

Memories of mask insanity will linger long after the mandates are rescinded. Even more disgraceful than seeing so many Americans submitting to these orders was watching this practice being taken to unimaginable extremes.

How many of you remember seeing folks wearing masks while inside their vehicles, nowhere near other people? One photograph circulated on the Internet showed the inside of a person's car where surgical masks were attached to cover all the air intake vents. Another social media video captured a woman shopping in a grocery store, face covering in place, surrounded by wheeled plexiglass shields that allowed her to navigate the store in perceived safety from the *China virus*.

More than three years from the outset of this ridiculous practice, I still occasionally see people wearing face coverings while shopping or exercising at a local fitness center, apparently oblivious to the oxygen depletion, bacteria buildup, and inhaled fibers.

In Oregon, Summit High School junior Maggie Williams was a couple of meters from the finish line of her 800-meter race when she started to lose consciousness and fell across the finish line, according to the Bend Bulletin. Williams's coach, Dave Turnbull, took issue with the fact that she was forced to wear a mask and suggested a lack of oxygen was responsible for her fall. Oregon was one of twenty states that mandated mask wearing during sporting competition, and Turnbull specifically criticized the Oregon Health Authority over the restriction.

A December 6, 2021, e-mail from Bruce Foster to the Nevada State Board of Health reported that at least sixty-nine athletes in a number of countries collapsed in one month, with several of them expiring. Problems such as cardiac inflammation are often the causes, one of the known life-threatening side effects of *China virus* vaccines, about which even the manufacturers themselves issued warnings.

Possibly the worst display of mask insanity was that of the Boston University men's basketball team obediently wearing red face masks while actively playing a game against Holy Cross in January of 2021. Boston University's policy on face coverings mandated that they be worn at all times in any shared spaces, which includes spaces off campus when a student is representing the university in an athletic event. Holy Cross, however, did not have such a policy on its campus, where the game was played, so their players did not wear masks. I found no reports of health emergencies with the BU team, but the ballplayers definitely gambled with their lives while competing under such duress.

These were just a few of the incredible number of examples that exposed the health risks to people wearing masks while participating in athletic competition. However, every incident involving oxygen deprivation during physical activity screams the following questions: *Why did these athletes even THINK of wearing obedience masks during sporting events, let alone complying with the insane mandates? Why in God's name didn't they refuse to compete? Were these athletes truly ignorant of the dangers they were confronting in these instances?* Most of the coaches and trainers certainly realized the madness being forced upon their players. School authorities and public officials should have been aware, likely were informed, but obviously were completely unconcerned about the athletes' health and well-being. They preferred to comply with the Leftists' narrative.

The *sheeple* who marched in lockstep with the mask mandates obviously had no idea of the history of forced mask wearing. Face covers were used in past ages to scorn, punish, and even silence critics of the state. This is exactly the mindset behind the *China virus*-related government mask mandates. Leftist officials were clearly aware that surgical masks did not prevent virus transmission; such is even noted on the mask packaging. If surgical masks don't protect against viruses, then certainly painter's masks, bandanas, scarves, and old pieces of cloth do not, yet people were regularly observed covering their faces with such items.

Forcing the public to wear masks in almost every venue had nothing to do with preventing virus transmission. It was a nefarious test to determine how well populations could be controlled. It stood to reason that authoritarian warning signs would quickly evolve into even more oppressive government control. Where is this going, you might ask?

Initially, sign postings read, CAUTION: A FACE MASK IS REQUIRED FOR ENTRY! Authoritarians then pushed vigorously for ones that stated, CAUTION: A VACCINE ID IS REQUIRED FOR ENTRY!

If allowed to continue, Leftists would have decreed: CAUTION: A DIGITAL ID IS REQUIRED FOR ENTRY!

There would have been no returning to normalcy if government authorities had been successful in implanting microchips into willing participants.

Time passed to reveal a December 19, 2022, Issues and Insights Techno Metrica Institute of Policy and Politics (I&I/TIPP) poll that indicated while a great many members of the Biden cabal may be listening to the science, they're not processing it as it regards the masking of children.

I&I intimated that what might partially account for the significant ideological split between the right and the left on the matter of masking kids is media and activist suppression of legitimate medical studies putting the efficacy of masking children in doubt.

Dr. Daniel Rauch, chief of pediatric hospital medicine at Tufts Children's Hospital in Boston, told *USA Today* that the *good news continues to be that COVID-19 is not a common problem for kids.*

A reasonable, honest exercise in research would uncover a fascinating history of people being forced to wear masks. Slaves across the globe have been masked to symbolically mark them as not having voices, being owned and controlled. In Africa, Asia, and North America, masks have been forced onto people for disciplinary reasons or to admonish them. Worst of all, mandatory masking is dehumanizing and humiliating and destroys people's individualities.

The ultimate insult to one's intelligence regarding this subject is people being photographed while wearing masks. How many of you have sent or received pictures of masked vacationers' faces in a wish-you-were-here greeting? A former coworker posted on social media a photo of his wife and him at Disney World. They were wearing black obedience masks and waving. How could I know who the subjects of the photo actually were? How could anyone know? When I posed the question of how in the world someone could possibly enjoy such an adventure while wearing face coverings, my friend responded, "So what? It's only a mask!"

Does anyone still believe that this insane mandate is no big deal? What the heck, it's only a mask, right?

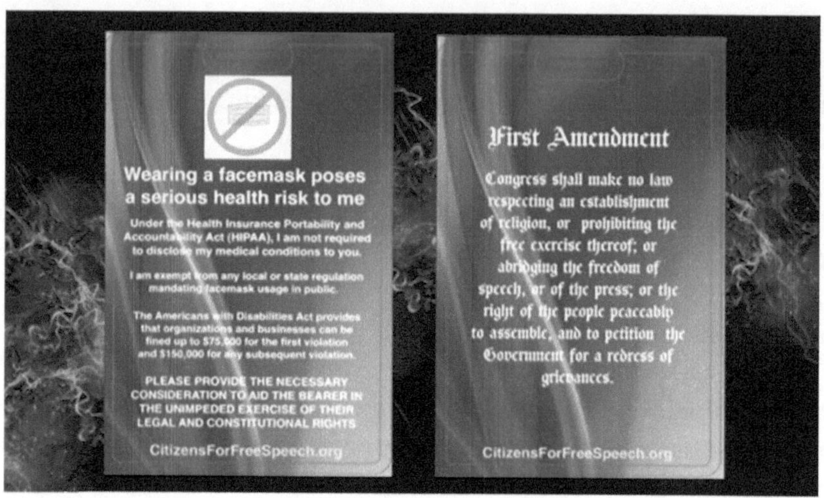

9

Insulting Our Intelligence

How many of you attempted to dine at your favorite restaurant during the *China virus* maelstrom? Were you required to wear a face mask simply to enter the building? Were you told to keep your mask in place until you were seated? Then, you were allowed to remove the mask in order to eat and drink, correct?

Once at their tables, diners ditched their masks, breathed the same air, could have spit food all over the establishment, and were allowed to partake in all the finery that was available, but managers then insisted that patrons reapply their masks while they exited the premises. Is this not a blinding insult to the intelligence of the average human being? The idea of mask-on/mask-off is bad enough, but such a practice inside a restaurant is beyond the pale and serves no purpose.

Do you remember browsing grocery store aisles and seeing directional arrows, painted footprints showing people where to stand, and an abundance of signs telling shoppers to remain at least six feet away from each other? Standing five and a half feet apart was not sufficient, I guess. A person could become a serial killer by hovering too close to others.

In several states, most notably California, government tyrants actually tried to impose mandates requiring people to constantly wear *obedience masks* within the confines of their own homes! Leftist Governor Gavin Newsom and his operatives unbelievably demanded that residents continue wearing masks even while eating, removing them only to ingest food or drink and then quickly replacing them. Is this an absurd are-you-shitting-me moment or what? Even though such a requirement could never be reasonably enforced, undoubtedly, many pansy liberals in *the land of fruits and nuts* complied like obedient sheep.

During the *plandemic*, it was common in the United States and other countries to hear political tyrants ranting about mandating *vaccine passports* to allow folks to move about freely and conduct their business. In some cases, unvaccinated people were denied access to goods and services, hospital care, and even employment. Fortunately, I was never confronted with such a mandate, but if I had been, the US Constitution and the Declaration of Independence are the only documents I would have presented to express my freedom!

Clear-thinking Americans quickly perceived the subterfuge being perpetrated on them by *The Collective*. Those with intestinal fortitude refused to relinquish their constitutional rights to the whims of lunatic Leftists. I, and many others like me, refused to wear *obedience masks*, rejected coerced or forced injections of any dangerous and untested *China virus* vaccines, and avoided patronizing business establishments that acceded to the government mandates of *social distancing* and oppressive, sometimes selective face covering.

Rational people questioned every comment and suggestion from government officials and their *fake news* lackeys and verified criticism of false narratives. Leftist media censorship of irrefutable facts grew exponentially in efforts to muffle common sense journalists and Internet bloggers who were presenting facts and analyses that exposed *The Collective's* lies and misinformation.

The conflict between dishonest purveyors of government manipulation and patriots trying to preserve America's freedoms brought about a time where intelligent people were being silenced so stupid people would not be offended.

The ideology of the Democrat party has been off-the-rails Leftist for generations, but radical, anti-American Marxists finally took operational control in 2020, wrenching it even further to the left, light-years beyond insanity.

The Democrat party continued to be the world's most successful hate group under the cloud of their *plandemic*. Leftist Democrats increased their efforts to attract poor people by convincing them to hate rich people. They prodded black people to hate white people, homosexuals to hate straight folks, feminists to despise men, environmentalist wackos to attack the internal combustion engine, celebrities to hate America, citizens to revile law enforcement and the Constitution, and bratty kids to dislike their parents.

The real secret of this party's success is that it attracts journalists who hate Republicans and therefore work tirelessly to convince people to vote for Democrats.

10

Subversion

The word *subversion* refers to a process by which the values and principles of a system in place are contradicted or reversed in an attempt to transform the established social order and its structures of power, authority, hierarchy, and social norms. Committing *subversion* can be described as an attack on public morale. *Subversion* is used as a tool to achieve political goals because it generally carries less risk, cost, and difficulty than does open belligerency. Furthermore, it is a relatively cheap form of warfare that does not require enormous amounts of training.

The corrupt, ideological, extremist political leaders who created and exacerbated the oppression of freedom and liberty during the *China virus* outbreak are unquestionably guilty of *subversion*. They manufactured crisis after crisis in order to foment fear and keep Americans off balance. Once a nation becomes locked into a crisis mode, a recovery is unlikely but for a civil war or foreign invasion.

Once a perceived emergency is firmly implanted within a society, it's not long before the population adapts to its aftereffects. The result is *normalization* of otherwise unacceptable authoritarianism.

There has been a method to the madness inflicted on humanity by a greedy, power-hungry cabal that lusts for a one-world government. A preponderance of evidence strongly suggests that the infestation of the *China virus* was the first stage in this plot. *The Collective* tested its ability to manipulate the American people through fear, unconstitutional mandates, and false promises of lifesaving vaccines.

Globalists share a mad craving for world population control, with themselves being the arbiters of life and death. The *China virus* provided the necessary fear but was not designed to be the exclusive agent for reducing populations. The scheme was to drive and in some cases force people into allowing themselves to be injected with one of several untested, experimental vaccines, whose side effects became the true killers. These drugs negatively impacted many people's natural immunity, triggered comorbidity issues, and damaged cardiovascular systems, while the conspirators vigorously blamed the virus for nearly every reported death, even ones not attributed to that disease.

Despite massive numbers of deaths and medical injuries, the most insidious by-product of the *plandemic* escaped notice by a large segment of the American population. The infestation led to mandates, lockdowns, and quarantines during the 2020 presidential election campaign. *The Collective* then managed to force the notion of mass voting by mail into the narrative. Their manipulation led to reams of ballots being sent to voters regardless of whether or not they legitimately requested absentee ballots, were registered to vote, or were even alive! From there came swarms of ballot drop boxes scattered about cities and towns and rarely supervised. Scores of harvesters were hired to collect countless containers of questionable ballots and to influence as many voter choices as possible. Consequently, the number of voters doing so in person was abnormally low.

On the campaign trail, Republican nominee and incumbent President Donald Trump appeared at dozens of nationwide rallies. His supporters thronged to these events by the hundreds of thousands, and he was on target to receive even more votes than he had accrued in 2016. His record of achievements for the betterment of the United States during his first term was exemplary, and he vigorously expressed his accomplishments.

The campaign of Democrat nominee, former vice president Joe Biden, was anemic, to say the least. He rarely addressed the public, and his visibility was near zero. During the eight years he served with former President B. Hussein Obama, his performance was lackluster, and his accomplishments were nonexistent.

However, as the votes were being tabulated, onlookers discovered huge discrepancies in the making. Numbers on electronic tote boards were mysteriously changing, lowering Trump's count while raising Biden's tally. It is unquestionably disconcerting as well as virtually impossible for a candidate's vote total to lower once the tabulation begins. Yet this happened to President Trump. Video recordings surfaced showing Democrat lackeys tampering with ballots, harassing Republican poll watchers, and producing hidden boxes of unsecured ballots. Election fraud ran rampant in 2020 to the Democrats' favor, and Biden was certified as the new president of the United States. President Trump unofficially received more than seventy million votes, a huge increase from his 2016 total. Joe Biden, who essentially did not campaign, allegedly received over eighty million votes. These numbers were highly suspect and did not reflect the particulars of this election.

The Collective was aware that Trump was a certainty for reelection. They knew that Biden had no chance of defeating Trump unless the Leftists engaged in a particularly discreet and precisely orchestrated theft of the election. They used an easily corruptible mail-in voting scheme to steal the presidency.

11

The First Impeachment of President Donald J. Trump

As if the American people weren't being agitated enough by the encroachment of the *China virus*, Leftist Democrats and anti-American zealots introduced impeachment proceedings against President Trump in January 2020. In fact, these hate-mongers began planning such an action only minutes after Trump's 2017 inauguration! However, this attack was driven by blind accusations and partisan hatred, without a shred of credible evidence.

The complainants were appropriately called *Never-Trumpers*, and their ranks included several prominent *RINOS*, (Republicans-in-name-only), from the political arena, academia, and journalism, along with a lockstep Democrat party and *fake news* media syndicate.

The protagonists claimed that Trump had solicited foreign interference to aid in his 2020 US presidential reelection bid. He was accused of urging authorities in Ukraine to investigate former vice president Joe Biden and his son Hunter, again, with no evidence and no substance to warrant an impeachment process. The US House of Representatives voted in the majority to impeach President Trump, anyway. Since when do facts and the rule of law matter to Democrats and cowardly, corrupt Republican ideologues?

On February 5, 2020, the Senate acquitted Trump on both articles of impeachment almost entirely along partisan lines. Mitt Romney of Utah was the only *RINO* senator to vote for the conviction and removal of the president.

Leftists have never feared President Trump damaging the nation. They've been terrified of his success. His every accomplishment marginalized the Left and degraded their control over voters. Always remember and don't ever forget that Trump is not *The Collective's* prime target. They want to control or destroy the American people. Trump is just standing in the way.

12

No Law, No Order

Violent crime per 100,000 residents jumped by 4.65% as police force levels decreased 2.1% in 2020 during the *China virus* pandemic, an Americans for Limited Government study of Federal Bureau of Investigation (FBI) Crime Data Explorer data from 1985 to 2021 shows.

The pattern generally indicates that to address the violent crime wave of the 1980s, surging law enforcement levels throughout the 1990s and early 2000s was effective at reducing overall violent crime rates, as one would expect, with greater numbers of officers resulting in fewer violent crimes reported. The mere presence of uniforms on the ground appeared to serve as a deterrent. Similar logic was applied to the Iraq War in 2007, when General David Petraeus led a troop surge in a counterinsurgency against Al-Qaeda forces that had taken control of parts of the so-called Sunni Triangle. As the forces increased, the insurgency was quelled, that is, until the United States withdrew forces under former President B. Hussein Obama, with the last military personnel leaving in 2011. Within two years, the Islamic State was reclaiming the territories that the troop surge had temporarily secured, and by 2014, Abu Bakr al-Baghdadi had declared a new caliphate. The United States commenced air strikes in 2014, but without ground forces, the Islamic State was not defeated. At its height, it controlled 33% of Syria and 40% of Iraq.

Finally, in 2017, President Trump used a combination of air power and ground forces to rapidly destroy the Islamic State. By December 2017, that faction had lost 95% of the territory that a lack of sufficient forces and security had allowed to grow.

In a war, it is necessary to hold ground, or ground will be lost. The lesson is power abhors a vacuum, so why would the United States create power vacuums in its own cities? That is exactly what the so-called Defund the Police movement envisioned in every state, city, county, and town across the country in response to numerous incidents where criminals have died while in police custody, including the death of George Floyd in Minneapolis in 2020.

In Minnesota, as police forces were reduced statewide in 2020 by 2.7%, violent crime shot up by a whopping 16.8%. Similarly, as police forces surged in the 1990s, violent crime dropped dramatically.

In Maryland, the opposite happened. When former Republican governor Larry Hogan came into power in 2015, he immediately expanded police force levels by 10.1% and then kept them steady throughout his administration, with further increases in 2018 and 2019. As a result, violent crimes dropped by 6.7% in 2018, 3.2% in 2019, and 11.9% in 2020.

In Oregon, similar increases in law enforcement personnel throughout the 1990s led to overall drops in violent crimes reported. A loss of personnel in the early 2000s led to an uptick in crime, followed by another surge that led to more decreases in violent crimes. In 2015, violent crime began increasing. By 2017, police forces increased by 8.1% and kept steady until finally, in 2020, the crime rate dropped.

The results in the state of Washington were much the same. Surges of police forces in the 1990s and early 2000s were effective at reducing reported violent crimes. A similar rise in violent crimes began in 2014, and eventually increasing police force levels from 2016 to 2018 led to ultimate drops in violent crimes committed in 2019 and 2020 by 3.8% and 3.2%.

It's pretty much like clockwork. As populations increase, more well-trained police are needed to maintain law and order. Recently, legendary *Punisher* writer Mike Baron even brought attention to this problem in his hit *Thin Blue Line* graphic novel. It is often a thin blue line of police officers that separates our cities from order and chaos. He's correct, but unfortunately, that line keeps getting thinner each year that force levels are reduced.

Ironically, as violent crimes predictably skyrocket when police force levels are reduced, there will be an increase in incidents that overworked and understaffed police officers must respond to, likely leading to an unfortunate rise in collateral damage. The individual circumstances obviously matter in determining whether individual law enforcement officers follow protocols, but department personnel levels appear to have a dramatic impact on the number of reported violent crimes.

In other words, when violent crime is increasing, governors, mayors, and law enforcement administrators may wish to employ the logic of surging police forces, with sheer numbers acting as a deterrent. That would lead to fewer violent crimes reported, needing fewer police responses.

Defunding the police and reducing force numbers will predictably lead to more violence and if allowed to persist to the extreme of anarchy, there will be no government to protect individual liberties and civil rights.

(By Robert Romano, *Daily Torch*, February 21, 2023. Robert Romano is vice president of Americans for Limited Government.)

13

Manufactured Outrage

It should be clear to anyone paying attention during this state of instability in our modern era that something is very wrong in terms of American society. It's not just about ongoing issues of political corruption and economic mismanagement but something much more threatening. The systematic derailment of the nation's culture, heritage, principles, history, and moral compass is well underway.

People must first understand the source of the problem. Who are the perpetrators, and why are they terrorizing the population? As much as some folks would like to believe that the current state of affairs is simply a natural consequence of social change, the reality is that the growing divisions in America are mostly engineered.

Two massive world wars in the twentieth century were enough to justify the creation of globalist bodies like the United Nations, the International Monetary Fund, and the World Bank, but not sufficient to convince the American people that abandoning national boundaries and national identity were necessary.

Americans have been historically resistant to increased centralization, even after decades of attempts by sinister forces to incrementally acclimate us to federal authority and naive notions of global citizenship. Clear-thinking folks do not trust such Utopian ideals because these concepts are used to sell the public on authoritarianism. Right before imposing mass censorship, secret arrests, Soviet gulags, Nazi cattle car trains, and genocide, manipulative political and military leaders preach *unity*, *equity*, and *fairness*.

The method in which collectivist propaganda is injected into a society depends on the type of culture being sabotaged. In the case of the United States, indoctrination of Leftist ideology has been quietly introduced through the educational system. Amply funded globalist groups like the Rockefeller Foundation and the Ford Foundation have invested heavily in appropriating American colleges, universities, and public schools.

The real abuse of power began in the late 1980s and early 1990s when Leftists deployed *deconstruction* as a weapon for political and social upheaval. Prior to this time, *deconstruction* was considered a mind game, a way to question traditional standards that were a basis for critical thinking. That definition changed dramatically in the 1990s.

The initial concept was to question binary notions in philosophy, but globalists and Leftists expanded it to question *everything* while engaging in active hostilities against the foundations of civilization. Leftists see structuralism as evil, and they despise anyone seeking to order society around rules, definitions, and principles that rely on intolerance of certain practices.

For Leftists, all rules and regulations must be undermined, and all behaviors must become acceptable for society to be integrated. Discrimination against anything is considered by them to be taboo because if people are free to disfavor, it allows them to separate, and if people are allowed to separate, then collectivism of thought can never be achieved.

Domestic terrorists took full advantage of the *China virus* confusion in 2020 and began expressing themselves by vandalizing, looting, and burning several major American cities. God forbid, these lunatic Leftist anarchists engage in any meaningful, civilized airing of grievances. Spearheaded by violent groups like *Black Lives Matter* (*BLM*, the crowd that chants, "Kill the cops," and "Pigs in a blanket, fry 'em like bacon!") and *ANTIFA* (the hypocritical anti-fascist bunch whose actions contradict their rhetoric), hordes of might-is-right terrorists began destroying property and assaulting innocent civilians with berserker rage.

Black Lives Matter was the biggest decentralized political and social movement against the incident of a police officer, causing the death of criminal suspect George Floyd, allegedly motivated by racism. The Floyd incident sparked major protests and riots all over the world against wrongly perceived police brutality and racial injustice. An estimated fifteen to twenty-six million took part in the *Black Lives Matter* protests.

Leftist instigators were unfortunately successful in planting the notion of *White Privilege* into the lexicon and ingraining it in the minds of the easily influenced.

Unbelievably, pansy Leftist mayors of cities like Portland, Oregon, Seattle, Washington, and Minneapolis, Minnesota, deployed law enforcement teams trained to stem the violence but then ordered them to stand down and simply observe the chaos. Even when rioters physically attacked officers, the officers were forbidden to engage their enemies. Criminals threw rocks, frozen water bottles, bricks, and other debris at law enforcement groups. They hurled bags of feces at officers' shields and, in isolated instances, actually discharged firearms.

The anarchistic *BLM* and *ANTIFA* violence lasted seven months and caused billions of dollars in damage. More than twenty people were shot and killed; thousands of law enforcement officers were injured; at least one hundred fifty federal buildings were vandalized; and hundreds of small businesses were destroyed.

Conservative Republicans, led by President Trump, condemned the rampages, but it was no surprise that Leftist Democrats and their lackeys in the *fake news* media encouraged the disorder! There was little or no outrage over all this destruction by Leftist Democrats like Kamala Harris and Nancy Pelosi who actually created funding sites to provide bail money for arrested rioters!

In contrast, the January 6, 2021, riot at the US Capitol, reportedly staged by Leftist infiltrators posing as Trump supporters, lasted only a few hours. Republicans and Democrats condemned that disturbance almost in unison!

It was only encouraged by fringe political groups. Most Republicans identified the protestors as similar domestic terrorists to those who vandalized cities the year before. Most Democrats alleged that these groups were White Supremacists, Ku Klux Klan members, and attendees of the Trump rally that day.

There was a police presence at the Capitol as there was in the besieged cities, but those officers appeared to take more action against the rioters than law enforcement did in Portland or Seattle. One person was killed at the January 6 disturbance, as opposed to the nearly two dozen deaths that occurred during the *BLM* and *ANTIFA* riots. Protestor Ashley Babbitt was unarmed, attempted to enter a barricaded opening to the Capitol, and was allegedly shot by Capitol Police Lieutenant Michael Byrd.

Fourteen police officers were reported injured. One federal building was damaged. No small businesses were destroyed. *The Collective*, however, orchestrated a national outrage over this event!

*REAL White Privilege: the ability to suffer whatever life
throws at you without blaming another ethnic group!*

14

An Authoritarian Manifesto

The Collective has been scheming for decades to fundamentally change the United States of America, long before B. Hussein Obama entered the political arena and uttered those infamous words. Unfortunately, they've been all too successful. Nefarious though their efforts have been, the unhinged Left injected their ideology slowly, patiently, in small increments, knowing that Americans do not react favorably to massive untimely changes in the relatively orderly running of their lives. The events that unfolded in the early months of 2020 provided *The Collective* with perfect camouflage for their social and political war against the American people.

Democrats and the *fake news* media ramped up their allegations that the United States is a racist, evil place. They pointed their gnarled fingers at honest, law-abiding citizens claiming that those people don't deserve the freedom and prosperity with which they've been blessed. Leftists included *revisionist history* in their arsenal, demonizing White people for the imagined crime of being White while encouraging Black people to be resentful and hateful toward White, Asian, and other non-Black individuals. This psychological operation caused even more damage to already-shaky race relations, further sowing distrust and division between ethnic and special interest groups.

Next, the Left created *destabilization* in the wake of the *China virus* infestation. Federal, state, and local government officials widely overstepped their authority and willingly violated the God-given, constitutional rights of Americans. They disrupted normal life by forcing thousands of businesses to close their doors and attacked people who objected to the damage being caused to the country's economy.

As soon as the American people became collectively imbalanced and confused, the Left used manufactured crises to strip away even more freedoms and institute additional demands, requirements, and orders. The *China virus* pandemic was of primary importance and demanded the most attention. Equally dangerous were the domestic terrorist attacks against cities like Seattle and Portland by violent anarchists from *ANTIFA* and *BLM*. Minneapolis was razed by mobs in response to the death of convicted felon George Floyd, allegedly while in police custody. Thugs assaulted innocent civilians, attacked police officers, ignited raging fires, destroyed buildings and small businesses, and vandalized and looted at will. Pansy Leftist political leaders not only allowed their cities to be destroyed, but they ordered battalions of law enforcement officers to stand by idly and simply observe the carnage, instead of preventing it. Many lunatic liberals expressed a mindset that destruction of personal property was insignificant as long as human lives were not at risk. Sadly, human lives *were* lost, and physical injuries appeared by the thousands as a result of these politicians' cowardice.

Lastly, *The Collective* forced the notion of *normalization* on the American people. Democrats, RINOS, and their media lackeys insisted, in no uncertain terms, that mask mandates were to be permanently implemented. Statues and monuments built to honor famous Americans and national events were to be removed if Leftists deemed them unworthy of public display. Sympathetic educators accelerated their efforts to indoctrinate students with Socialist, Communist, and Marxist group-think ideology.

Once government-ordered lockdowns expanded across the nation, a clear-thinking, observant person could easily detect the evil presence within such authoritarianism, an evil that would never disappear unless good folks fought back against it. The constitutional rights of Americans were and still are under attack. Fortunately, gallant patriotic citizens resisted the oppression from the outset and continue to do so.

> *One of the first things the Left does is take away the rights of other people to make their own choices!*
>
> —Thomas Sowell

15

Intolerable Hypocrisy

Leftists like to call themselves Liberals, but they're intent on abolishing liberty! They call themselves Democrats, yet they yearn for dictatorship! They demand to be called revolutionaries, but they want to make government all-powerful! They prevented people from visiting dying relatives in nursing homes and hospitals during the *plandemic* and stopped people from attending religious services but allowed marijuana shops and liquor stores to remain open! They blocked people from working at their jobs and operating their businesses but were tolerant of domestic terrorists burning down cities! They locked down the population for, in their minds, the greater good. Yet they allowed homosexual *Pride* members to make their own health decisions on lockdowns and vaccines! This hypocrisy is intellectually staggering to anybody paying attention to details! Is it really about *the science*?

16

The Greatest Fraud in Human History

Those who know the least obey the best!

In March of 2020, the Leftist mantra, energized by the lying media, was essentially *stay at home; wash your hands; do it for grandma!* By October 2021, though, government fascists escalated their oppression of American citizens by mobilizing the FBI to scrutinize and harass parents who were simply attending school board meetings and asking pertinent questions.

In Largo, Florida, the Pinellas County School Board was voting on a mask mandate after the emergency rule, imposed when schools opened that fall, expired. According to the *Tampa Bay Times*, twenty-five parents came to the meeting to argue against it, with some bringing along their children. During the event, a few parents decided to leave the building and apparently removed their masks while still in the hall. School district police officers asked one mother, Sam Stefano, to put her mask back on as she was exiting the building, beginning a heated argument that was captured on Facebook videos. Another mom, Kari Turner, who also had removed her mask, allegedly tried to defend Stefano. This part does not appear on video, so it's unsure why they eventually arrested Turner, but at one point, police pinned her thirteen-year-old daughter to the ground.

As time passed, more American parents began to voice their opinions and concerns at school board and local government meetings across the country. Their objections to mask mandates, Critical Race Theory programs, and Leftist indoctrination were usually met with scorn and condescension by board members. These parents presented themselves as well informed and articulate, for the most part, and their factual information often singed the nerves of authoritarian officials, to the point where committee chairmen ordered law enforcement officers to physically remove and, in some cases, arrest people who were merely exercising their constitutional right of free expression.

I continue to castigate every police official who ignored his or her allegiance to the Constitution and acceded to the demands of Leftist bureaucrats at the expense of the rights of law-abiding Americans!

Through a Freedom of Information Act (FOIA) request, the group Parents Defending Education (PDE) received e-mails indicating that Education Secretary Miguel Cardona solicited a letter from National School Boards Association (NSBA) officials to the Biden administration that targeted parents voicing concerns about education issues as potential *domestic terrorists*! The letter revealed that the White House was already actively engaged with NSBA President Viola Garcia and interim CEO Chip Slaven prior to the group's letter to Biden.

Subsequently, the Department of Justice (DOJ) announced that it was establishing a new unit to combat a perceived domestic terrorism threat, CNN reported. "We face an elevated threat from domestic violent extremists—that is, individuals in the United States who seek to commit violent criminal acts in furtherance of domestic social or political goals," Assistant Attorney General Matthew Olsen told members of the Senate Judiciary Committee. (Really? Somehow, this unit forgot to look at the groups that vandalized American cities!)

As in most, if not all, protests organized by clear-thinking, conservative-minded Americans, there are never instances of violence on their part. Many of the attendees even clean the protest sites and dispose of trash left at the events. Members of *The Collective* found themselves guilty of spreading lies once again!

Attorney General Merrick Garland called on the FBI to use its authority against parents who threaten or use violence against public school officials in a Monday memorandum. Garland said there has been a "disturbing spike in harassment, intimidation, and threats of violence against school administrators, board members, teachers, and staff." He said he is directing the FBI to work with each US attorney and leaders "in each federal judicial district" to discuss strategies to address threats within thirty days of his statement.

The Justice Department's memorandum did not specify what it classifies as a crime and did not immediately respond to the Daily Caller News Foundation's request for clarification on the matter. What a surprise?

The *China virus* will come and go, but *The Government* will never forget how easy it was to take control of your life; to control every sporting event, every classroom, restaurant table, and church pew; and even to decide if you're allowed to leave your house!

Former Trump administration Secretary of Housing and Urban Development, Dr. Ben Carson, told Newsmax that the *China virus* pandemic has been the "best mechanism government has had for controlling the people ever" and noted that it's contrary to the founding principles of America.

"Interestingly enough, when you think about the beginnings of our country, people came here so that they could be free, so that they wouldn't have the government's foot on their neck, mandating what they could and could not do," Carson, a retired neurosurgeon, said during an appearance on Newsmax's National Report. "This COVID situation has been the best mechanism government has had for controlling the people ever and they're very reluctant to let it go."

The authoritarian government tyrants who began micromanaging every American's life displayed stunning indifference to the plight of those infected with the *China virus*. Medical health professionals scrambled to develop treatments for this disease, using every tool at their disposal, but far too many doctors and nurses submitted to political directives, basing their decisions and diagnoses on guidelines from the Centers for Disease Control and Prevention (CDC) and the National Institutes for Health (NIH) regardless of professional disagreements.

Leftist conspirators widely publicized photographs and reports from the 1918 influenza pandemic, commonly known by the misnomer Spanish flu or the Great Influenza epidemic. This was an exceptionally deadly global health crisis caused by the H1N1 influenza A virus. The earliest documented case was in March of that year in Kansas, United States, with further cases recorded in France, Germany, and the United Kingdom in April. Two years later, nearly a third of the global population, or an estimated 500 million people, had been infected in four successive waves. Estimates of deaths range from seventeen million to fifty million, and possibly as high as one hundred million, making it one of the deadliest pandemics in history.

Old photographs of medical caregivers, patients, and onlookers wearing white cloth masks over their mouths and noses gave false credence to the perpetrators of the unconstitutional mask mandates of 2020. The 1918 face coverings did not prevent virus transmission any more than masks did over a century later. Researchers noted that many survivors of the influenza epidemic benefitted from therapeutic treatments, including an assortment of medicines available at that time, exposure to fresh air and vitamin D-inducing sunlight, and their own natural immunity. I have discovered no reports of any drugs being deliberately withheld from the sick during the 1918 pandemic, as restrictions on ivermectin and hydroxychloroquine were implemented in 2020.

In response to the *China virus*, some very distinguished and credible medical professionals and researchers promoted the use of ivermectin against the disease. This medication had been prescribed for a number of ailments, including malaria, for decades and was reportedly successful in nearly every usage. However, *The Collective* pushed another chemical called remdesivir onto virus victims, which generated multiple severe side effects resulting in permanent disabilities or deaths. Adding insult to injury, the powers that be actually prohibited the use of ivermectin by infected patients and forbade doctors and pharmacists from administering it. Why in the name of all that's holy would anyone physically prevent another person from availing himself of any legal and effective medication? Honest investigators eventually discovered that the manufacture of remdesivir was far more profitable for pharmaceutical companies than ivermectin would be, and a dastardly segment of the political elite stood to reap huge financial rewards for collaborating with the drug industry. These political tyrants and company executives valued profits over human lives.

Politico reported that the Biden administration was expected to stretch the *China virus* public health emergency again, potentially advancing the declaration past the November midterm elections and into next year. "So, they're going to continue trying to extend it just as far as people will tolerate, quite frankly, and they're not looking at science at all," Carson said. "Science tells us that viruses tend to attenuate so each iteration of it becomes a little weaker, but it also is more transmittable."

Carson added that viral weakening is the reason the US is currently experiencing an uptick in *China virus* cases but a low number of deaths. "It's a very different disease than what we had in the beginning, and they're not talking about natural immunity," Carson said. "People with natural immunity are doing just fine. They're doing extremely well, better than those who have been vaccinated."

Dr. Carson asserted that federal health officials don't want to hear about natural immunity. "Because if you acknowledge natural immunity, then you can't insist that everybody be injected," Carson said, referring to virus vaccine mandates.

17

Hostages

The heavy-handed unconstitutional mandates, directives to close most private businesses and churches, and the evaporation of people's God-given rights could not have been successful without an assortment of government enforcement agencies. Though there was little publicity or direct exposure, police officers and sheriff's deputies throughout the nation were ordered by corrupt bureaucrats to physically lock the doors of restaurants and fitness centers and, in some cases, arrest the proprietors, even though they had violated no specific laws. They simply objected to the audacity of pansy Leftists to suspend their livelihoods and eliminate the much-needed incomes of so many employees. Business owners received no due process of any kind. Their only right was the right to remain silent. How could this possibly happen in a constitutional republic and free democracy like the United States?

I developed a theory in response to seeing so many forced closings of legitimate businesses and named it the *Prisoner of War Syndrome*, with all due respect to every person who ever suffered as an actual prisoner of war. My question was, "Why would a large number of captives not attempt to overcome a significantly smaller force of captors?" I pondered the World War II history of the Japaneseforced Bataan Death March, the mistreatment of Holocaust victims by Nazi sadists, and other instances where small bands of armed assailants held much larger groups of victims as hostages. Why didn't the masses fight for their freedom by overpowering their adversaries? I believe the answer is that no one wants to take the first bullet in order to instigate a revolt. In one episode of the HBO series *Band of Brothers*, Captain Winters was concerned that Private Liebgott was angry enough to shoot German prisoners. Winters confiscated Liebgott's rifle ammunition, issued him one bullet, ordered him to march a handful of prisoners to a secure location by himself, and warned Liebgott, "If you shoot a prisoner, the rest will jump you. I want them all alive!" Winters was obviously concerned about a large group of prisoners overpowering a smaller guard detail, so the idea of captives taking such action is very real and likely happened somewhere, sometime in the forgotten past.

With my theory in mind, I wondered what would have happened if every officer on a police force, every business owner in a strip mall, every hospital employee, or every factory worker banded together and refused to submit to the illegal and unconstitutional mandates being forced upon them. I firmly believe that the Leftist authorities would have backed away from such shows of unity and significantly reduced their oppression. Unfortunately, taking the first bullet in these cases would have meant employees defying the mandates and risking termination of their careers, livelihoods, pensions, and benefits. They could have litigated unreasonable and illegal terminations, but they'd have been bogged down for ages during appeals processes, waiting for their dismissals to be overturned.

One more thought, if law enforcement authorities ordered officers to leap off of cliffs, would they do so? Would they be within their rights to refuse such an order?

There's no doubt that government tyrants threatened law enforcement officers with disciplinary action, up to and including termination, if they dared refuse direct orders. Officers were then forced to make painful decisions. If they acceded to the demands of their superiors, their paychecks and pensions would remain in place. At the same time, they would be violating the tenets of the US

Constitution and likely their own state's constitution, plus they'd be abandoning their oaths to protect and serve the public. *Their* jobs would be safe though.

If, on the other hand, law enforcement officers recognized that their orders were unlawful and exercised their obligations to refuse to obey them, they would be upholding the Constitution and the rights contained therein. The insane lockdowns would never have been implemented, the American economy wouldn't have been as drastically affected as it was, and the rule of law would have remained intact. On the downside, most of them would likely have been internally disciplined or terminated with loss of pensions and benefits. Government cronies trapped their enforcement servants in painful conundrums.

Reports during 2020 showed examples of officers from a few scattered police departments resigning, retiring, or transferring rather than complying with illegal orders, but the vast majority performed their duties as commanded. As a retired twenty-year law enforcement officer, I can sympathize with the quandary that enveloped these people. Most of them likely had families to provide for, considerable time invested in their jobs, and substantial pensions they could not afford to sacrifice. Being as principled as I am, I can state unequivocally that I would have refused unlawful orders, faced the consequences head on, and taken legal action to overturn any discipline or termination. I cast no aspersions on the officers who followed orders, even though I believe the American people would have suffered far less authoritarianism had the officers resisted illegal commands.

As egregious as the physical closings of so many businesses and institutions were, even worse were the myriad scenes of law enforcement riot control teams being sent to confront domestic terrorism in cities like Seattle and Portland and then forced to stand idly by while looters and vandals destroyed property and assaulted officers and civilians at will. Gutless Leftist mayors and governors vehemently refused to stop the destruction of their major cities. They chose to submit to the whims of anarchistic mobs rather than protecting their constituents.

While law enforcement officers were fighting their own local battles, far too many company managers injected the oppressive government mandates into the operations of their businesses. As the dangerous, experimental vaccines became available, policymakers began forcing workers to be injected with such drugs as a condition of employment. Arguably, the worst offenders of such regulations were hospital managers. As the spread of the *China virus* found its way into the year 2021, these Leftist lackeys preferred compliance with CDC, NIH, or other government agency recommendations over the well-being of patients and began suspending or terminating scores of clear-thinking doctors and nurses who recognized the hazards of *China virus* vaccines and refused to administer or receive any of them. Hospitals quickly became critically understaffed at times when patient admissions were skyrocketing.

An October 5, 2021, article by Sheila Flynn from https://yahoo-news.com reported that one North Carolina hospital system let go 175 unvaccinated employees. Another in Houston fired 150. United Airlines stood to lose up to 600 staff members. New York schools faced a potential shortage of nearly 3,700 workers. Firefighter unions from coast to coast battled serious discord within the ranks as many first responders refused to be vaccinated against the virus.

Within industries across the country, employer and government requirements prompted some skeptical workers to quit rather than receive the virus inoculation. Many were highly skilled. It's not easy to replace pilots and doctors, for example, in a matter of days, weeks, or even months.

From the sublime to the ridiculous, political poltroons like Governors Andrew Cuomo of New York, Gretchen Whitmer of Michigan, and Phillip Murphy of New Jersey issued orders to move elderly *China virus* patients from hospitals to nursing homes that were totally incapable of caring for them properly. They added to this oppression by preventing patients' families and friends from visiting their loved ones. The prevailing Leftist ideology claimed that isolating older virus patients would reduce the burden on hospitals and prevent more virus transmission. On the contrary, the persecution and confinement of Americans with growing medical concerns resulted in a greater spread of the virus and the unfortunate but likely preventable deaths of thousands of senior citizens.

18

Don't EVER Forget What They Did

Hiding behind the pretext of slowing the spread of the *China virus* and lowering the curve on charts indicating the disease's movement, fascistic political authorities in federal, state, and local governments magically turned the fifteen-day quarantine period they initially requested into *we don't know if it will ever end!*

They confounded or coerced the judiciary into becoming passive spectators and threatened law enforcement arms of government with disciplinary action or termination if officers refused to carry out unconstitutional orders.

Worst of all, these corrupt leaders created and expanded a conflagration of fear that subdued the vast majority of people into compliance. Expressing little or no courage and conviction, too many Americans sat quietly while government tyrants, with no legal authority, shredded the United States Constitution and people's God-given rights.

They closed our businesses, schools, churches, gun stores, and beaches. They banned parties, funerals, graduation ceremonies, nursing home and hospital visits, fathers in delivery rooms, and travel to certain states. They even designated what constituted a meal! In a most egregious display of hypocrisy and utter insanity:

> They allowed protests and riots.
> They allowed anarchists to co-opt cities.
> They allowed the storming of police precincts and assaults on peacekeepers.
> They allowed multiple attendance funerals only for people who fit their agenda.
> They allowed businesses to be destroyed and retail stores to be closed.
> They allowed statues to be vandalized and churches to be burned.
> They allowed the complete infringement of our liberty!

19

Collateral Damage

While Americans and, for that matter, the rest of the world were reeling under the endless assault by the *China virus* and the many authoritarian responses to the pandemic, agenda-driven ideologues took full advantage of the confusion to inject their mindset into the arena of ideas. As time progressed through 2020, observant people started noticing huge increases in pandering to lunatic fringe groups and special interest organizations.

White guilt liberals in the media quickly force-fed their audiences an inordinate amount of television programs, movies, and commercials that featured Black people, exclusively. I doubt that I was the only media consumer to recognize these changes. There was no public outcry claiming that Blacks were being discriminated against in the media, but with the attention of most Americans being consumed by the *China virus* crisis, it was a simple matter for pansy Leftists to push their unfounded agenda into high gear.

The homosexual lobby also took full advantage of the disorganized chaos. Advocates injected homosexual symbols and images into television commercials, a number of video productions, and even into children's entertainment. Crazed activists were not satisfied with simply solidifying same-sex marriages and themes into the public discourse. They took their derangement to astronomical levels by encouraging young people to change their biologically determined sexes medically and physiologically while browbeating society into accepting the absurd and unnatural beliefs that there exist more than two genders and that males can actually give birth. This is a classic example of a mindset I long ago termed *out-outrageousing*, where some off-the-wall folks engage in bizarre, abnormal behavior, and then others attempt to commit even more outrageous actions, for the sole purpose of receiving attention, even negative attention!

Consider how interconnected all these events are and how they're linked to *The Collective* and the globalist hunger for population control. The *China virus* was introduced to the world as a means to eliminate people who would be unable to recover from the infection. Instead of protecting people from the disease, the *China virus* vaccines actually became more effective instruments of population reduction than the virus was. Vaccine mandates accelerated the process by forcing millions of people to choose between their livelihoods and acceding to an experimental injection. Misdiagnosing and mistreating *China virus* patients by corrupted or intimidated medical providers led to significantly more deaths than should have occurred.

The explosion of homosexuality, gender identity, and sex-change surgeries into daily life exacerbated the decline of procreation rates in human populations. Let us not forget that the abomination of abortion advanced by Leftist ghouls also contributes to fewer human births.

The threat of nuclear war has been looming over the planet since the beginning of the Biden regime. Leftists salivate over population control through war and the riches they can accumulate by being part of the military-industrial complex.

Since President Trump's departure from the White House, concerns regarding shortages of food, water, gasoline, and other life necessities have skyrocketed. Increased prices of goods and services have been frightening. The Biden administration's weak and ineffective foreign policy, in conjunction with its extinguishing of so many Trump accomplishments, further endangers the United States and the American people.

20

Totalitarian Marxism

Governmental mandates like those implemented in 2020 can be found in Karl Marx's *The Communist Manifesto*, "Chapter 2: Proletarians and Communists," and they are exactly what today's Socialists and Marxists are trying to force on all of humanity. The phony *China virus* invasion served as a major distraction, opening the door for *The Collective* to ingrain these policies into everyday life.

Think back to what these tyrants actually imposed on the American people:

1. Abolition of property in land and application of all rents of land to public purposes.

    (Americans watched the CDC suddenly take control of landlords and tenants, generating an attack on personal and private property, income, and holdings!)

2. A heavy progressive or graduated income tax.

    (Americans continue to be burdened by taxes and have been for generations. Calvin Coolidge, John F. Kennedy, Ronald Reagan, and Donald Trump are the only presidents credited with implementing tax *cuts*!)

3. Abolition of all rights of inheritance.
    (*Democrats* want to reduce the cap on the estate tax to levels so low that it will be nearly impossible for average people to bestow their wealth, which they've already paid taxes on, to their children!)
4. Centralism of credit in the hands of the State, by means of a national bank with State capital and an exclusive monopoly.
    (*Democrats* want to massively increase the power of the IRS, to the point where that agency monitors and scrutinizes *everyone's* bank transactions of more than $600!)
5. Centralization of the means of communication and transportation in the hands of the State.
    (Big Tech controls social and corrupt media censorship!)
6. Gradual elimination of all the distinctions between town and country by a more equitable distribution of the populace over the country
    (*Democrats* want to devour the suburbs and relocate low-income housing into those communities!)
7. Free education for all children in public schools.
    (Leftist brainwashing, from grade school to public colleges!)
8. Millions of illegal alien invaders are swarming over the United States/Mexico border at the invitation and urging of Biden and the corrupt Democrats. These aliens are from all corners of the Earth, not just Central America; most are not vaccinated or even examined for medical issues; and then the CDC issued a warning about a possible measles epidemic! Biden and the Democrats have orchestrated all of this *intentionally*!
9. Suddenly, the FAA refused to allow FOX News drones to video record the masses of illegal alien invaders at the US southern border, after allowing these flights for quite some time. More censorship!
10. Democrats want to *nationalize* election laws in order to turn the country into a California-like one-party state. They want to *fix* the elections, so they never lose!

11. Academic freedom is under attack, unless you're a Leftist!

12. There is no free press in this country. The *New York Times*, *Washington Post*, major TV networks, CNN, and MSNBC are all propaganda organizations, appendages of the Democrat party and the *Deep State*!

13. Class warfare and redistribution of wealth based on race or anything the Democrats can use to exploit and turn against the American people!

14. Balkanization, rich versus poor—this is how they plan to push through their massive spending bill that will bankrupt our children, grandchildren, and generations to come.

15. Critical race theory; indoctrination of children to be racists. Whether they're White, Black, Brown, or Red, they're supposed to feel superior or inferior or hate some other group because of skin color.

16. War on private property and capitalism, climate change, and Green New Deal all came to light in the 1970s as a de-growth movement. Attack energy and fossil fuels, expand the police state (*Big Brother* is watching), IRS, massive bureaucracy, more regulations and penalties, more fines and mandates, and more control—just look at how corrupt government officials have oppressed some Americans because of their negative reactions to the *China virus* agenda.

17. According to the Free Beacon website, more than 250,000 Americans have died under Biden's watch, yet he accused President Trump of causing EVERY SINGLE CHINA VIRUS-RELATED DEATH nationwide.

18. Biden inherited three national vaccines and successful therapeutics from President Trump. A quarter of a million Americans have died during his regime, but Biden blames the unvaccinated. Statistics say that 76% of Americans have received a *China virus* vaccine, 24% have not. What percentage of that 24% have natural immunity and antibodies? The CDC won't provide such information, so it's really more than 76% that are protected.

19. And the madness that is the *Crazy Uncle Joe* fascist empire marches on to even greater heights of failure, courtesy of the *Democrat Election Fraud* of 2020 and the legitimate votes of lunatic Leftists!
20. Never forget that Democrat mayors and other government officials sent law enforcement SWAT teams to close down churches and barbershops while allowing domestic terrorists to loot and burn American cities unmolested!

The four steps to totalitarian Marxism

1. Demoralization (saying the United States is a racist, evil place; saying we don't deserve what we have, revising history)
2. Destabilization (shutting down businesses, stopping normal life from resuming, attacking those who think for themselves, dismantling the economy)
3. Crisis (COVID-19, climate change, George Floyd, ANTIFA riots)
4. Normalization (mandating masks to go anywhere, statues and monuments gone, schools indoctrinating students with Marxist group-think ideology, people relying on government to pay their bills)

All four of these steps were implemented in 2020! If you aren't worried about the future of your country and your children's future, you should be! Ever since the lockdowns started, many people felt an evil presence in the country, and it won't go away unless we fight back!

21

For the Truly Ignorant

(Remember: The word *ignorant* is defined as "not having enough knowledge, understanding, or information about something." It does not necessarily mean *stupid*!)

Just about everything *The Collective* and Big Tech tried to conceal concerning *their* definitions of *China virus* misinformation turned out to be true in the end, according to an op-ed from the *Wall Street Journal*.

With the blessings of the federal government, social media companies like Twitter and Facebook blocked key information about lockdowns, face masks, and the vaccines. Had more people been able to access this information, perhaps fewer of them would have succumbed to the disease.

Accurate history and verifiable facts confirmed that the *China virus*, itself, killed very few people. Most deaths were related to fear and hysteria, forced social isolation, and mandates to wear *obedience masks* over people's breathing apertures.

Improper hospital protocols, like applying ventilators and administering remdesivir to infected patients, quite likely killed thousands, if not millions, of people. Big Tech did its part to keep these events hidden by labeling credible warnings shared through the Internet as disinformation.

"Legions of doctors stayed quiet after witnessing the demonization of their peers who challenged the COVID orthodoxy," the *Journal* reported about the matter. "A little censorship leads people to watch what they say. Millions of patients and citizens were deprived of important insights as a result."

"Health authorities and TV doctors insisted young people were vulnerable, demanded toddlers wear masks, closed schools, beaches and parks, and were loath to contemplate crucial cost-benefit analysis. The economy? Mental health? Never heard of them."

There was mass censorship of factual information about the drugs ivermectin and hydroxychloroquine (HCQ), which deprived populations of simple, safe, and effective remedies for the *China virus*.

Meanwhile, corrupt government bureaucrats funneled an astonishing *$6 trillion* into all sorts of other remediations, including the ruinous Operation Warp Speed, afflicting tens of millions of people with debilitating side effects and, in some cases, death.

These virus vaccines were determined to be certifiably useless in stopping the spread, but that never deterred the authoritarians or the *fake news* media from constantly advocating them. The massive public health costs of force-feeding vaccinations have only just begun to manifest.

The worst year for excess mortality, in fact, was 2021, the year of the vaccine. Prior to that, relatively few people died from contracting the actual *China virus*, even though the dishonest media swayed viewers and listeners into believing that individuals were collapsing in streets far and wide from some fabricated contagion.

"Excess mortality in most high-income nations was worse in 2021 and 2022 than in 2020, the initial pandemic year," the *Journal* explained. "Many poorer nations with less government control seemed to fare better. Sweden, which didn't have a lockdown, performed better than nearly every other advanced nation."

"After navigating 2020 with relative success, young and middle-age healthy people in rich nations began dying in unprecedented numbers in 2021 and 2022. Health authorities haven't focused enough on this cataclysm of premature death from non-COVID heart attacks, strokes, pulmonary embolisms, kidney failure and cancer."

Despite all the censorship, the truth is being reported and received, thanks to the power of the Internet. Authorities recognize this, which is why they are attempting to suppress even more free speech.

> "Digital censorship is their response to this crisis of authority," is how the Journal op-ed put it.
>
> Censorship prevents the truth from being shared, which can lead people to make deadly, misinformed decisions. (Ethan Huff, July 12, 2023)

I pose an honest question to the throngs of no-information people who salivate over the prospect of living in a United States of Socialism: *Which part of this lifestyle are you looking forward to the most, eating zoo animals, like in Venezuela; being shot for criticizing the government, like in Cuba; or having the national economy completely tank, like in Greece?*

A person who submits to Socialism is essentially admitting that he or she can't compete in the real world. Such an individual concedes, "I'm willing to give up my liberty, my religion, and my dreams as long as the state takes care of me."

For all the Never-Trumpers and Trump-haters, what did you hate the most about his presidency? Was it the absence of major wars around the globe? Was it relative peace in the Middle East? Could it perhaps have been the strong American economy? What about the total absence of economic inflation? Did you hate the growth of 401(k) accounts? How about the rise in stock market profits? You couldn't have hated the price of gasoline, could you? Did you not want a secure strategic petroleum reserve? You couldn't possibly hate lower taxes or the strong American dollar, hmm?

Once a Socialist government provides people with basic utilities, it's then able to decide when to turn them on or off. Once the state provides free education, it can control curriculums and ultimately people's careers. Once Socialists provide food, they can choose how much people can eat. Once they regulate housing, they control where people live. Once a Socialist government pays for healthcare and medicine, it can control whether people are valuable enough to stay alive. Once Socialists convince people to accept gun control, there is no way to prevent them from achieving everything listed above!

Accepting Socialism is accepting failure.
It's the complete opposite of the American representative
republic and all of the opportunities available
within a democratic system of government.

22

What REALLY Happened on January 6?

At the Save America Rally on January 6, 2021, President Trump, thousands of his supporters, and millions of Trump voters showed that they were light-years beyond outraged at the stolen 2020 presidential election. The evidence of fraud was widespread and irrefutable. A huge audience rallied at the US Capitol to listen to the rightful president's address. What was the state of the nation at that time?

Gasoline prices averaged $1.93 a gallon. There was ZERO inflation. America's supply chain was running effectively. The US economy was the strongest it had been in fifty years. The border with Mexico was relatively controlled and secure. The Taliban weren't armed with billions of dollars in US military equipment. There were enough available workers to fill the nation's labor needs. Stock market numbers and 401(k) accounts reached all-time highs. Interest rates were at record lows.

Inside the halls of government, though, Democrats, Never-Trumpers, RINOS, and even Vice President Mike Pence ignored the shouts of election fraud, fortified their subversive coalition, and sat idly and silent while the Democrat-controlled Congress certified *walking gaffe machine* Joe Biden as president.

The first Trump impeachment can be traced back to nineteen minutes after he was inaugurated on January 20, 2020. He was convicted by a cowardly partisan House of Representatives based on no evidence of any wrongdoing. Fortunately, the Senate was unable to accumulate enough votes to remove him from office. That wasn't enough for all the deranged Trump-haters who shoved their smear machine into an even higher gear, impeaching him for the second time on January 13, 2021, one week before his term was to expire.

Ten Republican representatives voted for the second impeachment, the most pro-impeachment votes ever from a president's party. This was also the first presidential impeachment in which the majority caucus voted unanimously for impeachment.

The House of Representatives of the 117th US Congress adopted one article of impeachment against Trump for incitement of insurrection, stating that he had orchestrated the January 6 attack on the US Capitol. These events were preceded by Trump's attempts to overturn the 2020 presidential election, as well as his pushing of voter fraud theories on his social media channels before, during, and after the election. A single article of impeachment charging Trump with incitement of insurrection against the US government and lawless action at the Capitol was introduced to the House.

Trump addressed a gathering of his supporters at the Ellipse in Washington, DC, on January 6, the day Congress was counting the electoral votes. During the rally, Trump and other speakers insisted that the election was stolen, based on mountains of credible evidence. He used the word *fight* in an effort to boost the morale of his followers, made an analogy to the sport of boxing, and suggested that American patriots had the power to prevent Joe Biden from taking office.

When Congress convened to certify the electoral votes of the presidential election, some members of the crowd crossed the Mall and stormed the United States Capitol in an alleged attempt to prevent the tabulation of votes and to protest against Biden's stolen victory. Most Trump supporters demonstrated peacefully, but a number of agitators, quite likely infiltrators hired to damage the optics of the rally, illegally entered the Capitol and gathered on its eastern and western sides, including on the platform constructed for Biden's inauguration. Five people died as a result of the incident. Capitol Police Officer Brian Sicknick returned to his division office after engaging the rioters but later died of a stroke. Kevin D. Greeson was standing with Trump supporters when he suffered a heart attack. Roseanne Boyland was allegedly overwhelmed by the crowd, but evidence showed she was suffering from drug addiction. Benjamin Philips, the founder of a pro-Trump website called Trumparoo, also died of a stroke. Only one fatality, Ashli Babbitt, resulted from direct violence, allegedly shot by a Capitol Police lieutenant. A number of mistakenly perceived improvised explosive devices were found on and near the Capitol grounds. Four other police officers mysteriously committed suicide in the days and months after the riot.

FBI agents worked about 16,000 more hours during the pay period of the Capitol riot than they did during the pay period of the 2020 riots that hit Washington, DC, according to documents obtained by the Heritage Foundation's Oversight Project through the Freedom of Information Act.

Payroll records for FBI agents in the Washington, DC, field office show they worked a total of 86,262 hours in the January 4 to January 17, 2021, pay period, during which the Capitol riot occurred.

By contrast, during the May 25 to June 7, 2020, pay period, when the *Black Lives Matter* and *ANTIFA* riots were occurring in the District of Columbia, payroll records show that FBI agents worked a combined total of 70,367 hours. It was on May 29, 2020, at Lafayette Square in Washington, DC, that rioters gathered near the White House and set fire to the historic St. John's Episcopal Church.

The FBI did not provide information about how many of the more than 86,000 hours were spent on January 6 cases alone, according to the Heritage Oversight Project, which is suing for more transparency.

In the first week of the 2020 riots, about 150 local and federal law enforcement officers were injured in the District of Columbia.

The 2020 riots ultimately incurred $2 billion in property damage nationally and resulted in at least nineteen deaths, according to news reports.

During a speech at the event, President Trump told his supporters, "We love you. You're very special," restating his well-founded claim of election fraud, and then asked them to return home. Congress reconvened later and ultimately certified the electoral votes in the early morning hours of January 7. Trump then released a statement asserting that there would be an orderly transition of power on Inauguration Day, even while continuing to expose evidence that the election was stolen from him.

At the conclusion of the trial, the Senate voted 57–43 to convict President Trump of inciting insurrection, falling 10 votes short of the two-thirds majority required by the Constitution, and Trump was therefore acquitted. Seven Republican senators joined all Democratic and Independent senators in voting to convict Trump, the largest bipartisan vote for an impeachment conviction of a sitting or former US president.

Truth does not mind being questioned.
A lie does not like being challenged!

23

The Stolen Election!

One striking definition of stupidity is watching a president of the United States create the strongest economy in American history—during a pandemic—and then choosing to vote for the other guy in the next election!

Folks need to understand that Democrats aren't *denying* that there was election fraud; they're just saying that no one can *prove* it!

As harmful and disruptive as the *China virus* infestation and the subsequent declared state of emergency were, they provided excellent camouflage for arguably the most sinister aspect of the Leftists scheme, stealing the 2020 presidential election in favor of the Democrat candidate.

Follow the breadcrumbs. Millions of Americans were quarantined in homes, healthcare facilities, and other shelters. Public gatherings were discouraged and, in some cases, forcefully prevented. Many business transactions were limited to teleconferences, e-mail, and telephone conversations. How were election officials going to organize the voting during the upcoming election? Simple; they installed ballot drop boxes in large-population areas. The Leftists mailed bundles of ballots to as many names and addresses as they could obtain, and then Democrat operatives harvested them.

What about the legitimate concerns for security and accountability of the ballots? Observant voters across the nation witnessed countless procedural irregularities and blatant lawlessness. Several truck drivers detailed to fair-and-balanced media sources and election officials that they were ordered to illegally deliver loads of ballots across state lines. Television viewers watched video recordings of Republican poll watchers and overseers being physically restrained from entering voting sites and performing their lawful duties in Philadelphia by what appeared to be Pennsylvania State Police officers. Surveillance video evidence showing Leftist agents tampering with ballot drop boxes began appearing on a few honest cable news programs and on the Internet. Democrat poll workers were captured on film producing previously hidden cartons of ballots after the close of voting hours. The election thieves initiated a cleverly complex and stunningly successful operation. They engineered hands-on manipulation of physical election ballots and rested assured that the *fake news* media would control and censor any incriminating information.

I believe that if the American electorate majority had voted with their heads instead of with their glands, President Trump would have won reelection with landslides of popular and electoral college votes that would have been too massive to be overcome by election fraud. However, on November 3, 2020, this electorate majority was a living definition of stupidity. The Trump campaign machine roared to life again, as it did in 2016. His operatives organized scores of political rallies across the nation, in nearly every state, and every event drew tens of thousands of Trump supporters. Throngs of cheering crowds filled live venues, while countless thousands more enjoyed watching video coverage. President Trump's media advertisements were crisp and clear. He adhered to his campaign promises while successfully accomplishing his first-term agenda, the *PEOPLE'S* agenda.

Under President Trump's leadership, the United States became energy independent for the first time in decades. The American economy was robust, unemployment levels reached all-time lows, and inflation was essentially nonexistent.

The stock market achieved astronomical numbers, and consumer confidence was at a seventeen-year high. Trump reduced or eliminated hundreds of crushing business regulations previously imposed by a Democrat-controlled White House and Congress.

The Trump administration actively enforced US immigration law, significantly slowing the illegal alien invasion across the Mexican border, and advanced construction of an effective physical barrier to stymie unauthorized intruders, further securing America's southern border.

Throughout Trump's presidency, there was relative peace in the world, thanks to his firm and aggressive foreign policy. President Trump eased tensions between the United States, Russia, and China. He forced the North Korean communist government to refrain from its militaristic posturing and halted that country's testing of long-range missiles over the Sea of Japan. President Trump sanctioned Iran over its nuclear weapons and guided missile programs.

The *New York Post* reported that the average price of gasoline on January 20, 2021, the day of Biden's inauguration, was $2.39. The average gasoline price on June 7, 2022—18 months later—was $4.86, according to the American Automobile Association (AAA).

Republican President Herbert Hoover was the first to donate his salary beginning in 1929. Donald Trump also donated his presidential salary in the form of grants to the National Park Service, Department of Education, Department of Health and Human Services, and Department of Transportation.

When was the last time a DEMOCRAT president used his salary in such a manner? John F. Kennedy did so, starting when he was a congressman and then a US senator. Though Kennedy was a liberal Democrat ideologue, he also recognized the upside of common sense, conservative ideals.

The Democrat push for a 2020 presidential candidate was nothing less than chaotic. More than a dozen Socialists, Leftists, Communists, and America-hating narcissists engaged in a free for all of mudslinging, slander, and libel against each other. When the flatulence finally dispersed, former vice president Joe Biden was crowned the Democrat candidate. However, the Biden campaign began at a snail's pace and then slowed to virtually a standstill.

President Trump energized millions of rational people across the country with his political events, rallies, and speeches. Sensible voters recognized and appreciated Trump's accomplishments, honesty, and America-first approach to leadership.

Joe Biden was scoffed at for essentially running a campaign from his basement. Biden's political gatherings and personal appearances were marred by painfully low attendance. While Trump was drawing tens of thousands of supporters, Biden followers numbered in the hundreds. Biden's campaign messages were woefully weak and unenergetic. His alliteration was so inarticulate that his handlers retreated him from stages and microphones and replaced him with surrogate promoters.

President Trump's policies produced magnificent accomplishments to the benefit of all Americans. It was infinitely preferable to the Democrat doom-and-gloom scenario of high taxation, government control, burdensome regulations, anemic foreign policy, and apathy toward the growing crime rate. Prognosticators felt nothing less than a Trump landslide victory. Trump supporters were in total agreement. How could anything else happen?

Then, a dark fog began to overwhelm the voting. The Democrat party used the confusion and chaos of the *China virus* lockdown to overstep the boundaries of election rules and laws. First came the installation of ballot drop boxes in cities and towns across the nation. Leftist Democrats convinced the electorate that depositing their ballots in these containers was akin to voting by mail, despite the accepted design of absentee voting being reserved for people who were actually unable to appear at a polling place.

Going from the sublime to the ridiculous, Democrats and their operatives frivolously distributed bundles of ballots to the general population. This resulted in many individuals collecting more than one ballot, while others received none.

The danger to the United States is not Joe Biden. It is a citizenry capable of entrusting a man like him with the presidency. It will be far easier to limit and undo the follies of a Biden presidency than to restore common sense and good judgment to a depraved electorate willing to have such a man as their president. Biden is merely a symptom of what ails America. Blaming the prince of fools should not blind anyone to the vast confederacy of fools that made him their prince. Our republic can survive a fool like Biden, but it is unlikely to survive the multitude of fools that made him their president.

24

Beyond 2020

We weren't crazy.
We weren't making things up.
We weren't selfish.
We weren't killing people.
We weren't hurting others.
We weren't lying.
We weren't just being stupid.
We weren't ignoring the actual science.

We were vilified.
We were fired from our jobs.
We were excluded from society.
We were discriminated against.
We were mocked.
We were blamed.
We were thinking critically.

We were RIGHT!

After pouring out thousands of advertisements, journalistic reports, and so-called expert testimonies that drowned the American people in lies and disinformation, *The Collective* apparently realized that honest, fact-based research from rational truth-seekers ultimately exposed the *China virus* vaccine fraud. Statistics began detailing the enormous numbers of deaths and health problems being caused by the assortment of experimental vaccines and eyes of the public started opening. Leftist authoritarians and their operatives in the pharmaceutical industry appeared content in the knowledge that lawmakers had indemnified these companies from any responsibility for adverse product side effects. However, cracks began appearing in this immunity shield as victims of dangerous, untested vaccines were finding some success with malpractice claims through the legal system. Time will tell the final story of this search for accountability.

On March 17, 2023, NEWSTARGET journalist Ethan Huff reported that e-mails from 2020 were discovered, proving that COVID PCR tests being pushed by government authorities on the masses during the Wuhan coronavirus pandemic were nothing more than a scam.

In September 2020, Professor Martin Neil received a handful of anonymous e-mails that unequivocally proved the fraudulent nature of these tests, which were never designed to detect viruses. "Some of the test sequences are found in the human genome itself," according to one message. Also, the cycling threshold of PCR testing kits was almost uniformly set too high, resulting in numerous false-positive readings. Were these kits initially approved or certified for such testing? They were not.

One of the most stunning bits of information was the gene sequencing that Dr. Christian Drosten used in his blueprint COVID testing system, which was shared worldwide. Drosten, who was credited with inventing the screening system for COVID, never isolated the virus nor even had access to it.

A number of reports explained, "Instead, he downloaded the virus RNA sequence from a Chinese database. Drosten subsequently created the first commercially available RT-PCR screening kit based on this genome."

Chinese researchers later claimed the isolated virus sample became unusable shortly after uploading the sequence, so they destroyed all remains. (Food for thought: How can PCR tests search for the *China virus* if the disease has never been isolated and proven to exist?)

PCR tests are fake, just like the *China virus*! The anonymous e-mails explain that in addition to some of the primer sequences coming from the human genome itself, other portions of it come from an unknown source in seawater.

What this all means is that COVID testing was a ruse and the virus itself appears to have been fake as well. The entire thing was an operation designed to instill fear, paranoia, and obedience to the government.

It would have been timely for Neil to have published these e-mails once they were received, but neither he nor anyone else did so. The truth is that there was never any new, sinister coronavirus, based on this smoking gun evidence.

Instead of being truthful, *The Collective* kept this information from the public and continued pushing its fraudulent virus testing scam. Government Leftists stoked fear by alleging new waves of the virus and claimed that the very same tests designed to determine *China virus* infection were somehow detecting variants, even though none of the variants had ever been isolated, either. Laboratories analyzing COVID test results abandoned the standard World Health Organization (WHO) guidelines for identifying positive test results, making it abundantly clear that the entire charade was a *scamdemic* in every sense of the word.

The Expose's Rhoda Wilson wrote about the e-mails, "This evidence again pointed to the cross-reactivity and non-specificity of the PCR test. It looked to be designed to pick up, well, anything that you might want it to detect." Rather than find residue of SARS-CoV2 virus fragments, the tests seemed to be quite efficient at finding *any* coronavirus. They may have worked perfectly well, but just not for their specific purpose. Keep in mind that the common cold is a coronavirus, which means the tests were likely just picking up the seasonal sniffles and then used to scare and coerce people into being vaccinated. Such was clearly the plan all along.

One sign that the vaccine pushers were scrambling to cover their behinds came on October 31, 2022, from an article in *The Atlantic* by Emily Oster titled "Let's Declare a Pandemic Amnesty." The author implored, "We need to forgive one another for what we did and said when we were in the dark about COVID!" News flash: Clear-thinking people were NEVER in the dark about COVID! The initial reports of the contagion smelled fishy simply because of the panic-laden rhetoric the accompanied it. As time progressed and political poltroons flexed their authoritarian muscles more and more, the stench of their scheme became overpowering. People on the right side of history are usually fighting for freedom, not for oppression, censorship, or re-education. Those who know the least obey the best.

Back in August of 2021, *The Atlantic* published four similar articles taking just the opposite stance on the *China virus* vaccines.

1. "The Anti-Vaccine Right Brought Human Sacrifice to America!"

   (Since last summer, the conservative campaign against vaccination has claimed thousands of lives for no ethically justifiable purpose!)

2. "Unvaccinated People Need to Bear the Burden!"

   (Beyond limiting the coronavirus's flow from hot spots to the rest of the country, allowing only vaccinated people on domestic flights will change minds too!)

3. "Vaccine Refusers Don't Get to Dictate Terms Anymore!"

   (People who opt out of shots shouldn't expect their employers, health insurers, and fellow citizens to accommodate them!)

4. "Some Americans No Longer Believe in the Common Good!"

   (They now are only thinking of themselves!)

Fast-forward a year, and it turns out that the clear-thinkers were right all along. The unvaccinated did not spread the disease. Natural immunity was always the best defense. The untested, experimental vaccines were ripe with dangerous and deadly medical side effects. The naturally immune folks continued on with relatively virus-free lives, while great numbers of people who submitted to vaccines and multiple booster injections found themselves infected or reinfected with the virus.

This is only one example of lunatic Leftist hypocrisy. The vaccine promoters in government, and the corrupt media couldn't tout the drugs' safety and effectiveness enough once the vaccines became available, but in the aftermath of their ignorance and arrogance, they scrambled to cover their asses by offering insincere apologies and begging for forgiveness. They knew damned well that this entire *plandemic* was a nefarious scheme designed to thwart President Trump's anticipated reelection, keep the American people dazed and confused, and dabble in a little population control.

Many new studies offer even more proof lockdowns were deadly! Clear-thinking folks who didn't march in blind obedience to Leftist Democrat overseers knew this whole event was fraudulent from the beginning. That's why so many of us resisted the authoritarianism!

In hopes of containing the pandemic, Americans nationwide were forced to suffer through lockdown orders, closed schools, and shuttered workplaces in the spring of 2020. In Democrat-controlled areas, many of these restrictions lingered into 2021. Yet they didn't work. Untold numbers of people contracted the *China virus* anyway, more than a million Americans died because of the disease, and ironically, the major spreading of this virus happened in homes. The restrictions themselves obviously produced deadly consequences.

A report by Casey B. Mulligan and Rob Arnett published in the journal *Inquiry* found that non-COVID deaths were highly elevated above normal expectations in the United States in 2020 and 2021. The report indicated that over this period, approximately 97,000 Americans died annually (not including COVID deaths) above the baseline trend, a statistic known as *excess deaths*.

These included 32,000 deaths from heart disease and hypertension, some of which may have been exacerbated by the disruption of healthcare services and healthy lifestyles caused by *China virus* restrictions. Deaths from obesity-related illnesses, drug overdoses, and alcohol-related events were all 12,000 to 15,000 above expected trends. All these factors were heavily influenced by the way the unconstitutional lockdowns forced social isolation, sedentary lifestyles, and mental health issues.

The study concluded, "Point to a historic, yet largely unacknowledged, health emergency. COVID-19 is deadly, but so were the draconian steps taken to mitigate it."

Excess deaths were categorized by age and offered clarity to the findings. Among victims aged eighteen to forty-four, total *excess deaths* (more than half of which were non-COVID related) were highly elevated. "While largely unharmed by COVID, their aggregate mortality rates increased 26 percent above previous trends," the study reported. "This is larger than the percentage jump in deaths for senior citizens, where the COVID toll was largely concentrated, but has received scant notice," due to increasing Leftist censorship.

People within the eighteen to forty-four age group were always at very minimal risk of dying from the virus, but the fact that they saw so many excess deaths suggests that they were more affected by the restrictions, even though the restrictions were allegedly imposed to protect other groups, specifically, the elderly.

Not every death was directly attributable to *China virus* restrictions, but common sense and basic comparisons dictate that many certainly are. For example, Sweden, which took a much more hands-off approach to COVID lockdowns, actually saw fewer *excess deaths* than expected. In fact, they experienced no increase at all.

While many governmental public health *experts* still refuse to acknowledge the facts, the Mulligan/Arnett study proved that lockdowns had deadly consequences. This is not just an outlier; it's one of many that reached similar conclusions.

As order slowly returns to life in the United States, Americans are left to ponder an ugly truth. Government oppressors quarantined people, destroyed their livelihoods, shuttered their schools, and frightened them into huddling in their homes. Not only did these lockdowns have fatal consequences, but they also caused immeasurable anguish for those who didn't die, and they failed to contain the

China virus. The self-aggrandizing experts and tyrannical officials who pushed these failed policies must be held accountable for their injustice.

Some people never grow. They never learn their lessons. They never recognize their mistakes, they never acknowledge their faults, and they never admit they were wrong. They will never apologize, and their behavior will never change!

25

The REAL Dictators

All of the Leftist Democrats and two-faced RINOS who called President Trump a Hitler-like dictator throughout his entire term need to get grips on themselves. Their audacity to wrongly accuse Trump of malfeasance that *they* actually committed is light-years beyond hypocritical. These truisms are all ingrained in the historical record:

1. TRUMP never censored free speech. Lunatic Leftists did!
2. TRUMP never used the media to silence his political opposition. Lunatic Leftists did!
3. TRUMP never threatened to confiscate citizens' firearms. Lunatic Leftists did!
4. TRUMP never threatened to put people who disagreed with him into reeducation camps. Lunatic Leftists did!

In reality, the voters who elected so many crazed Leftist politicians are directly responsible for their representatives' actions and transgressions! Take a long hard look at the *hypocritical, dog-faced pony soldier* (a Biden quote) staring back at you from a mirror!

Here are the top five facets of American lives that Leftists and the Biden Regime want to permanently eradicate:

1. Your immune system
2. Your small-to-medium-sized business
3. Your children's morals and values system
4. Your concept of democracy
5. Your spirituality

The *China virus* pandemic was never the problem—it was *The Government's* solutions to it that destroyed everything!

The first step in liquidating a people is to erase its memory. Destroy its books, its culture, its history. Then have somebody write new books, manufacture a new culture, invent a new history. Before long, the nation will begin to forget what it is and what it was.

—Milan Kundera

26

They're Not Just Wrong…
They're DANGEROUS!

Too many people hold a mindset that the rift between Republicans and Democrats, Conservatives and Liberals, and Right versus Left is widening due to innocent personal opinions, civil disagreements, and honest mistakes. Nothing could be further from the truth. Republicans and Conservatives—two names that are not necessarily synonymous—are as prone to committing errors as are any other human beings, but their modi operandi generally include working to improve the livelihoods of all Americans; providing for the common defense, which includes prevention of illegal alien invasions; equal application of and equal justice under the law; minimal-sized government; the lowest amount of taxation possible; and honoring the tenets of the US Constitution. *The Collective*, which includes most Democrats, Leftists, Socialists, Marxists, Communists, and anarchists, historically despises and abhors Republicans, Conservatives, the Constitution, organized religion, law enforcement, the military, and the rule of law. They strive to create gargantuan government entities, oppressive laws and regulations, fascistic population control, and outrageous taxation.

Do you still think that Leftists are not dangerously wrong but are simply misunderstood? Read on!

Liberalism is an ideology that is the gateway drug to Leftism. Conservatism is a way of life. The difference between modern Liberalism and Conservatism is the first one believes that government is owner and distributor of freedom and rights, while the other maintains that government exists to protect the rights and freedoms Man is born with.

The Collective and their willing accomplices in the *drive-by* media are unquestionably and verifiably dangerous to life in the United States. Their accurately recorded historical commentary and activity expose the risks that Leftists pose to our representative republic. Consider these irrefutable facts:

1. *The Collective* rejects an assertive US foreign policy. They pander to communist dictators and rogue nation terrorists in the manner of former British Prime Minister Neville Chamberlain, who passively capitulated to Adolf Hitler's Nazi regime!

2. They oppose free enterprise, advocating massive government regulations to oppress the business community. Think back to the illegal lockdowns of commerce beginning in 2020!

3. Leftists demand open US borders and illegal alien invasions. They palpitate over the notion of illegals becoming a permanent underclass of Democrat voters!

4. *The Collective* is beholden to radical special interest groups. Authorities turned blind eyes to domestic terrorist organizations like *Black Lives Matter* and *ANTIFA* that destroyed American cities, while insisting that the greatest threat to the country was Right-Wing activism!

5. They shun traditional values and advocate the homosexual agenda, sanctuary states and cities harboring illegal aliens, and so-called woke social justice warfare!

6. Leftists vigorously attack the Constitution's Second Amendment and the existence of firearms in general

because an unarmed population is much easier to control than an armed one!

7. They kneel at the altar of big government, they're free-spenders who ignore deficits and the national debt, and they are totally unprotective of the freedoms and God-given rights guaranteed to Americans in the Constitution!
8. They salivate over the opportunity to redistribute the income of Americans as a quid pro quo to special interest groups, enticing them to vote for Democrat political candidates!
9. They also never met a tax they didn't like, from excise and estate charges to endless fees, levies, and tolls!

It is a historical fact that high taxation forces workers to become much more frugal, which, in turn, lessens the flow of revenue into the US Treasury. Republican Presidents Calvin Coolidge, Ronald Reagan, and Donald Trump and Democrat President John F. Kennedy all recognized the folly of overtaxation and took steps to reduce burdensome taxes. The result each time was a noticeable increase in revenue production. It's a simple law of economics.

The cabal of lunatic Leftists outwardly hates organized religion, particularly Christianity. They are less hostile toward Judaism and rarely address Hinduism or Buddhism, but they take great pride in absolving the Islamic faith and its radical terrorists of from any wrongdoing. How fair is that? How hypocritical is it?

The Democrat presidential administrations of Bill Clinton, Barack Obama, and Joe Biden weaponized organizations like the Department of Justice, Federal Bureau of Investigation, Central Intelligence Agency, Internal Revenue Service, Bureau of Land Management, and others to harass, intimidate, threaten, and, in some cases, arrest and prosecute persons and groups they disagreed with, all in the name of control.

This kind of persecution has appeared throughout human history in Soviet Russia, Communist China, Nazi Germany, Fascist Italy, Imperial Japan, and any number of dictatorships that rose and fell throughout the millennia. *The Collective* aligns itself with every one of these ideologies and philosophies, applications of which have resulted in the deaths of hundreds of millions of people.

On the other hand, America's Founding Fathers rejected monarchies and oligarchies in favor of a representative republic in the United States. Which type of government do *you* prefer?

Elected and appointed political authorities and jurists possess human failings, which can lead to making poor or irresponsible decisions, some of which have had far-reaching consequences. Government corruption and judicial malpractice are not novel happenings, but the frequency of injustice in these practices has skyrocketed.

In 1998, President Bill Clinton was impeached by the US House of Representatives but was not convicted or removed from office by the Senate. Irrefutable evidence of lying under oath and obstruction of justice warranted Clinton's impeachment. The wail emanating from his fellow Democrats and supporters was that his crimes *didn't rise to the level of impeachment*. In Clinton's case, the rule of law was fairly applied.

In 2019 and again in 2021, President Donald Trump was impeached by the House of Representatives and like Clinton, the Senate refused to convict him or remove him from office. In the first instance, *The Collective* accused President Trump of *abuse of power* and *obstruction of Congress*. Democrats alleged that Trump unlawfully solicited Ukrainian authorities to influence the 2020 US presidential election. The charge that spawned the second impeachment was *incitement of insurrection* in the aftermath of the January 6 incident at the US Capitol. In both cases, there was not a shred of factual, verifiable evidence of wrongdoing presented to support the charges against the president, zip, zero, nada! These impeachments were irrefutably political witch hunts, vain attempts to remove Trump from the presidency because his administration was resoundingly successful in derailing *The Collective's* schemes and returning the United States to economic prosperity, energy independence, and effective foreign policy.

It's clear to anyone who's been paying attention to the social and cultural instability in our modern era that something is very wrong in terms of American society. The issues of political corruption and economic mismanagement are troublesome enough. I'm pointing to something much more dangerous: the systematic derailment of our culture, heritage, principles, history, and moral compass. Americans are suffering a vicious devouring of the very sinews that hold civilization together. We must first understand the source of the problem and determine who or what is causing it and why.

As much as some people would like to believe our current state of affairs is a purely natural consequence of social change, the reality is that the growing divisions in America are mostly engineered.

In the 1950s and early 1960s, the world was trying to recover from the horrors of World War II and the Korean Conflict. World War I had ended forty years earlier, but its memories were still fresh in millions of minds as well. The United States entered into an age of relative prosperity. It was at this time that multiple organizations posing as philanthropic institutions sought to satisfy their insane hunger for globalism. Two massive wars and one *police action* were shocking enough to justify the creation of bodies like the United Nations, the International Monetary Fund, the World Bank, and the Bureau of Industry and Security, but not enough to convince the populace that abandoning national boundaries and national identity was a good thing.

Americans have long resisted further centralization, even after decades of attempts to incrementally acclimate us to federal authority and naive notions of global citizenship. Many of us do not trust such Utopian ideals primarily because it is always these same concepts that are used to sell the public on authoritarianism. Right before they implement mass censorship, secret arrests, gulags, cattle car trains, and genocide, the powerful elitists love to talk about unity, oneness, equity, and fairness.

The way in which collectivist propaganda is injected into a society often depends on the type of culture being sabotaged. In the case of the United States, it has been quietly introduced through the educational system. Globalist groups such as the Rockefeller Foundation and the Ford Foundation have been heavily involved in hijacking

American colleges, universities, and public schools using the massive funding at their disposal.

The real power grab occurred in the late 1980s when *deconstruction*, as a weapon for political and social upheaval, was widely introduced into Leftist circles. Before then, *deconstruction*, derived from the work of the philosopher Jacques Derrida, was often thought of as a mind game, a way to question long-held standards that acted as a basis for critical thinking or philosophy. In the 1990s, it became something else.

Derrida advocated questioning binary notions in philosophy. Globalists and Leftists expanded it as a concept for questioning everything and even engaging in active hostilities against the foundations of civilization. Leftists see *structuralism* as a target, and they despise anyone seeking to order society around rules, definitions, and principles that rely on discrimination of certain behaviors.

For Leftists, all rules and protections must be undermined, and all behaviors must become acceptable in order for society to be homogenized. Discrimination against anything is considered by them to be taboo because if people are allowed to discriminate, then that allows them to separate, and if people are allowed to separate, then collectivism of thought can never be achieved.

Morality is a binary based on right and wrong. It is the most vital binary for human survival, and without it, our species would self-destruct. This seems to be exactly what Leftist puppeteers want. They see traditional morality as restrictive and oppressive, another binary that must be eliminated. They propose moral relativism instead: the idea that conscience is merely a product of social conditioning and that right and wrong, truth and lies, and good and evil are based on personal preferences.

This is, in fact, the recipe for ultimate evil. It is the philosophy of pure chaos. When individual conscience becomes the enemy of society because it is considered an act of discrimination, then only evil can prevail.

Leftist activists are easily duped, highly flawed, and cowardly people. They want society to see their greatness. They want adoration and respect but do not want to put in any effort to earn it. They have images in their minds of who they are, but those images don't mesh with reality. So they try to enforce the images rather than admit they need improvement. *Deconstruction* allows them to break down long-valued standards of merit, morality, and accomplishment. With deconstruction, *anyone* could be idolized, even the vilest fanatics on the planet.

This is why there can be no diplomacy or reconciliation with groups that value Leftist philosophy and *deconstruction* ideology. The intent is to poison the culture well. The purpose of Leftists is to destroy the world because they consider it oppressive to their narcissism. Globalists exploit that narcissism and use Leftists as a battering ram to wreak havoc. Through chaos, they hope to erect a new world order in which all values, all principles, and all morals are dead and psychopathy becomes normal.

The only alternative is to wipe Leftist ideology and *deconstruction* off the face of the Earth before it's too late. One cannot reason with a monster. One can only erase that monster from existence.

"WE, THE PEOPLE"

The Coronavirus will come and go, but a corrupt government will NEVER forget how easy it was to take control of your life. Tyrants controlled every sporting event, classroom, restaurant table, church pew, and even the freedom of people to leave their own homes!

27

Conclusions

What should have been a finest hour for medicine, science, and democratic governments became a colossal failure, both from a professional point of view and from the reality of the violation of fundamental freedoms and the loss of public trust.

These failures were not the fault of honest, dedicated medical professionals who made Herculean efforts to properly address the *China virus*. They were caused by inexcusable negligence on the part of corrupt politicians and healthcare malefactors. Agencies that acceded to *The Collective's* demands included the World Health Organization (WHO), whose mission is to work "worldwide to promote health, keep the world safe, and serve the vulnerable"; the Food and Drug Administration (FDA); and the United States Centers for Disease Control and Prevention (CDC), all of which fixated on the *China virus* while neglecting their responsibilities to promote overall health and protect the public.

The fanatical approach and the draconian measures employed against a disease that by any measure was considered mild to moderate and no different from the influenza epidemics of the 1960s and 1970s caused profound harm to millions of people and created aftershocks that will likely be felt for generations to come. The end result is a significant social fissure plus economic and political instability.

It would be stunningly naive to think that it was simply tunnel vision and managerial blindness that caused these failures and not ravenous appetites for power, control, and wealth.

One exhaustive investigative research report proves undoubtedly that the *China virus* pandemic was, in fact, planned out over several decades within the highest echelons of the US government. An extremely powerful *shadow government* directed every facet of the enormous lobbying efforts and legislative processes required to execute such a crime wave against the American people. To coin a phrase, the barbarians have been inside the gate and operating with impunity, likely since the Federal Reserve Act of 1913 was implemented.

The evidence is so compelling based on the extraordinary chronology of official governmental acts and essential legislation from start to finish. Well-concealed perpetrators designed a perfect combination to overwhelm the American people. The launch of the *China virus* bioweapon was obviously the first punch that deftly set up the weaponized vaccine second punch. The ultimate intention was the global administration of an exceedingly injurious and often lethal vaccination in order to depopulate planet Earth.

Most people, me included, were unaware of the complexity of the heinous plan that was unfurled in 2020. The sudden appearance of a new disease or epidemic is not a novelty in human history, but the instigators of the *China virus* malaise promoted the greatest media blitz of all time through their willing accomplices in the press. It did not require much effort to instill fear and trepidation into global populations. In the modern age of instant worldwide communication, consumers can be easily overwhelmed by a tsunami of misleading information.

Many folks are conditioned to trust government authorities and organizations. Others are fearful of retribution for failing to abide by government edicts. Few are the people who have the intestinal fortitude to question policies and mandates that they find objectionable.

Once authoritarians ingrain a sufficient amount of angst into a population, it becomes a simple task to force most people into compliance, no matter how extreme the demands might seem.

Government leaders first deceived Americans into believing that the *China virus* was the most infectious disease and calamitous disaster ever to hit the planet. Some crazed Leftists predicted a doomsday scenario or an extinction-level event. Folks were then told that a population-wide fifteen-day quarantine would stifle the spread of the virus. That time period quickly expanded indefinitely. Then, the lies that wearing face coverings and standing six feet away from other people would protect against contamination were mass advertised.

Skeptical Americans started questioning these government practices and resisted their implementations. In response, the authoritarians mounted a campaign of threats, intimidation, and, in some cases, violence to achieve their goals. The United States began drifting toward third-world country status.

Always remember and don't ever forget that these oppressive tactics were used by *The Collective* against American citizens: Corrupt bureaucrats mandated private businesses and companies to enforce mask-wearing and social distancing orders, under penalty of fines or arrest. Leftist tyrants commanded law enforcement agencies to physically impose compliance, and most officers obeyed orders for fear of incurring disciplinary action or losing their jobs. Local government leaders threatened service providers such as physicians, dentists, and dining establishments with license revocations in the event they failed to abide by and enforce the mandates.

Then came the *China virus* vaccination requirements. Many terrified people began scrambling to obtain these injections, believing the disinformation from the CDC and other government agencies. A considerable number of people were hesitant to ingest any untested, experimental vaccine. Since the goal of *The Collective* was to subject every person to one of these drugs, authorities pressured businesses to force their employees to be vaccinated or be terminated from their occupations.

While Americans were embroiled in an alleged national health emergency, Leftists covertly schemed to steal the 2020 presidential election. Trump derangement syndrome was more infectious and debilitative to these subversives than the *China virus* could ever be. They capitalized on quarantines and a huge reduction in personal interactions to aggressively advocate exclusive voting by mail. They utilized illegal ballot drop boxes, ballot harvesters, mass ballot mailings, cross-state ballot transportation, and corrupt poll workers to directly manipulate votes. No sane person could have imagined that a widely accomplished incumbent president would lose his reelection bid to a politically impotent challenger.

The manipulators succeeded in subjecting the world's populations to a dangerous disease that took countless lives. They introduced vaccines that could reach even more people. Eventually, those drugs would prove to be more destructive than the virus. Leftist Democrats subverted a presidential election and replaced an effective, patriotic leader with an America-hating administration that eradicated most of the incumbent's beneficial achievements.

Ultimately, *The Collective* and their population control co-conspirators across the planet created ideal conditions through which they could eliminate large numbers of Earth's human inhabitants. The *China virus* took a terrible toll on victims who suffered from comorbidity health problems. The various vaccines killed thousands outright and continue to claim victims over time. Leftist glorification of homosexuality and gender reversal negatively impacted birth rates. The change in US presidential administrations obliterated previously successful foreign and domestic policies, bringing the world closer to nuclear war and more violent population control.

One plausible theory suggests that global elitists desired to remove large swaths of human beings in any way possible and then redirect the remaining resources to their own coffers. I wonder if the perpetrators considered how many people would be needed to remain alive in order to provide menial labor, operate essential machinery, and tend to the needs of those privileged few?

With Satanic precision, *The Collective* fundamentally changed not only the United States but the entire world. We are witnessing the disintegration of the rule of law. Innocent people are being wrongfully prosecuted, while the guilty are often ignored. Radical domestic terrorists continue to vandalize cities at will, maim and kill civilians, and attack law enforcement officers, all with the blessings of pansy Leftist authorities. *Wrong* suddenly became *right*, while *right* became *wrong*.

28

Epilogue

Four particular types of people emerged from the rubble of the *China virus plandemic*. Each is easily identifiable. It is quite likely that you know friends and family members who fit nicely into one of these categories:

1. Those who believe the Leftist narrative and continue to comply with it.
2. Those who know the narrative is bullshit but comply with it anyway.
3. Those who are waking up to the lie and are beginning to refuse to comply.
4. Those who KNEW the narrative was bullshit from the beginning and refused to partake in the lie.

The reality that some people close their minds, refuse to consider verifiable facts and information, and behave like partisan ideologues is incomprehensible to clear-thinking folks. It's evident that these devotees hold fast their loyalty to Leftist Democrats, believing that *their* authorities would *never* lie to them or steer them in the wrong direction. There is likely no cure for this type of psychological dysfunction.

The *sheeple* who were aware that the Leftists were lying to them but complied with the illegal and unconstitutional mandates are a curious lot. They were forced to make uncomfortable and often painful decisions. Too many of these victims were required to constantly wear *obedience masks* under penalty of termination from their jobs. They were ordered to wear face coverings simply to obtain goods and services. In extreme circumstances, employers and government officials demanded that workers receive the experimental *China virus* vaccines or lose their employment. It's difficult to expect every American to stand on principle at the risk of losing his or her livelihood and even harder to condemn them for complying with oppressive mandates, but historically, Americans have shown enough resolve to confront a revolution, a civil conflict, two world wars, and scores of national crises with courage and righteousness. There was obviously a severe shortage of these traits during the phony pandemic.

It is refreshing to learn that large numbers of people around the world are emerging from their comas and joining the ranks of the noncompliers. Once again, it's difficult to comprehend why these folks took so long to recognize the tyranny and fascism being thrust upon them, but I suppose better late than never is acceptable in this regard.

We, who knew from the start that the entire *China virus* debacle was fraudulent; who knew that the mask and vaccine mandates were unconstitutional; who knew that Leftists were on a warpath to remove President Trump from office and to depopulate the planet; and who knew that if we didn't stand up for truth, justice, and the American way, our country would be reduced to a third-world hellhole in short order, refused to wear face coverings except in the most extreme circumstances. We defied the vaccination mandates. We contracted the *China virus* and survived it by means of healthy immune systems while sharing as much factual, verifiable information as possible with the nonbelievers. Our task was difficult, tedious, and frustrating, but we never sacrificed our principles or our patriotism, and we've emerged victorious.

This macabre series of events has been devastating humanity for more than three years, and it is still far from ending. Don't think for a second that *The Collective* (Leftists, Socialists, Marxists, Communists, et al.), the Deep State, Globalists, One-World government tyrants, and population control freaks have disassembled their agenda and faded into obscurity. They perpetrated the greatest hoax against humanity, and their efforts were stunningly successful. Resistance to their oppression continues to rise in conjunction with the amount of information being uncovered and exposed to the public, but their hellish ideology will never be extinguished until it is universally rejected and denounced.

I chose to focus my attention on the initial year of this ongoing saga to keep alive the painful memories of national and worldwide government authoritarianism, the grief and suffering perpetrated by sinister egoists, and the ruination of so many innocent lives. Fortunately, my family and I have been blessed with enough intelligence and common sense to maneuver through and survive the onslaught.

The saddest aftershock is a stunning indictment of present-day humanity. Far too many people abandoned courage, sensibility, and principle, choosing instead to accede to the unlawful, irrational manipulations by government authorities. This global exercise was a test of people's resolve, and Americans as a society failed miserably. The steadfastness that created our independent nation and sustained the country through a civil war, economic depression, and scores of bloody conflicts has gone the way of the Dodo. I remain convinced that if a supermajority of Americans had outright refused to be quarantined; defied unconstitutional mandates; rejected experimental vaccines; forcefully kept businesses, churches, and schools open; raged against a fact- and evidence-based presidential election fraud; and exercised logic, common sense, and intolerance of oppression, much of the death and destruction wrought by this sinister plot would have been prevented.

Future historians, at least the honest ones, will record details of the *China virus* pandemic, the fraud that pilfered the 2020 US presidential election, and the nefarious population control scheme in their proper contexts. Hopefully, their analyses will be spared the corruption of censorship, misinformation, and disinformation in favor of facts and the truth. As always, time will tell.

Meanwhile, there are endless lessons to be learned from the vast array of failed responses to the events of 2020. Among them is that an important and profound expression of God-given rights is vital. Too many of the world's residents have no shields against fascism and tyranny, but Americans are protected and blessed by the greatest governing document ever created, the United States Constitution. We must all utilize it wisely, express it often, and continue to remind the short-memory crowd of its importance!

The freedoms you surrender today are the freedoms
your grandchildren will never know existed!

ABOUT THE AUTHOR

Joe Calitri, a seventy-two-year-old retiree from Massachusetts, lived in Florida for twelve years and has been comfortably settled in Texas since 2016. Creative writing has been his forte and passion, and his conservative commentaries have been published in newspapers, Internet blogs, and on social media platforms for decades. He has written two politically themed books, another detailing his career in law enforcement, and has produced three original music CDs. He is motivated to continue expressing truth supported by evidence in his compositions and hopes to expand his reading and listening audience.